YOU WILL BE MY WITNESSES

You Will Be My Witnesses

Meditations for the Easter Season
(Sundays and Weekdays)

Bishop Michael Campbell OSA

ST PAULS

The Scriptural quotations used in this volume are the author's own
translation from the original Greek.

Cover image: *The Resurrection* by Aidan Hart
Cover design by DX Imaging

By the same author and published by ST PAULS:
A Shoot from the Stock of Jesse
A Time to Seek the Lord
Mary, Woman of Prayer
The Greatest of These is Love
The Way of the Cross with Saint Paul

ST PAULS Publishing
187 Battersea Bridge Road, London SW11 3AS, UK
www.stpaulspublishing.com

ISBN 978-0-85439-810-2

A catalogue record is available for this book from the British Library.

Set by Tukan DTP, Stubbington, Fareham, UK
Printed by Gutenberg Press, Malta

ST PAULS is an activity of the priests and brothers
of the Society of St Paul who proclaim the Gospel
through the media of social communication.

To the memory of
Father James McEvoy (1943–2010),
priest, scholar, friend.

*The precious bond of human friendship is delightful
because it draws many souls into unity.*
St Augustine, *Confessions*, Bk 2.2,10.

CONTENTS

Introduction

The reflections in this book, drawn from the Church's scriptural texts for the Easter season and entitled *You Will Me My Witnesses,* are the completion of a liturgical trilogy by the author. *A Shoot from the Stock of Jesse* covered the season of Advent, and *A Time to Seek the Lord* that of Lent. All three volumes have the same, single purpose: that of being a help to Catholics who attend Mass on a daily basis and who wish to acquaint themselves beforehand with the Scripture readings of the day. Many people are unable to attend church daily but may still be able to experience something of the flavour of the particular liturgical season by following the scriptural reflections in these volumes.

Each liturgical season has its own unique atmosphere and rhythm, but the season of Easter represents the climax of the Church's year, with the resurrection of Jesus Christ at its centre. The readings from Sacred Scripture for Eastertide, which the Church lays before us, describe the beginnings of the first Christian community and its rapid expansion in response to its experience of the risen Christ and the promised Holy Spirit. The fundamental scriptural text for the Easter season is the second volume of the Evangelist Luke's work, the Acts of the Apostles. In this work we are taken step by step along the road of the early Church's journey, characterised both by setbacks and progress. The apostles Peter and Paul are destined to play a prominent part in this story. A wide and carefully chosen selection of gospel texts serves to enhance this pivotal liturgical season.

If the believer and reader of these pages comes to experience something of the Easter joy and hope which characterised that first Jerusalem community of Christians, then the work of the author will be amply repaid.

+Michael Campbell OSA,
Bishop of Lancaster

Octave of Easter

Readings: Acts 10:34, 37-43; Colossians 3:1-4,
(1 Cor 5:6-8); John 20:1-9

They have taken the Lord out of the tomb,
and we do not know where they have laid him.
John 20:2

The opening reading for Easter Day, from the Acts of
the Apostles, depicts Peter, in the house of Cornelius
the Roman Centurion, giving a little catechism of the
life, death and resurrection of Jesus, and the saving
significance of these events. Cornelius and his household
would represent, as it were, the first-fruits of the non-
Jewish world to be baptised and receive the gift of the
Holy Spirit. Crucial to Peter's short discourse was the
crucifixion of Jesus of Nazareth and his being raised from
the dead by the power of God the Father. Peter and his
fellow apostles were eye-witnesses to these astonishing
and incredible happenings, as well as to the whole of
the public life of Jesus Christ. This passage from Acts
contains the kernel of what would constitute the faith of
the Church for all time, founded upon the testimony of
those first apostolic witnesses. The Creed we say at Mass
and the baptismal promises we will renew today are a
development of the address of Peter to Cornelius and his
household.

The reading from Colossians presupposes baptism, in which the Christian mysteriously dies on the cross with Christ, is buried along with him, and raised to share with him the glorious new life of the resurrection. In his letters the apostle Paul insisted on the profound change wrought by baptism in the life of the Christian. Our past, sinful life has been crucified and exists no more. Consequently, our outlook and moral behaviour from now on should be orientated towards Christ seated in glory at the Father's right hand. The wonder of Christian baptism points us towards the future and the victorious reappearance of Christ, when the glory conferred on us through baptism and now hidden will be revealed in all its splendour.

Saint Paul's words to the Corinthians have an Easter-Passover ring to them, and are highly appropriate for Easter Day. In the Exodus story (Ex 12), a new start was envisaged for the Israelites, enslaved in Egyptian bondage, with the baking of the unleavened bread and the discarding of the old yeast. The sacrificial lamb and the saving power of its blood would form the centrepiece of the Passover feast. The Apostle here applies these paschal images to the Christian community in Corinth: Easter and the sacrifice of Christ, the lamb of God, on the cross mark a completely new beginning for the individual and for the Christian community as a whole. The old, selfish and sinful manner of living belongs to the past. A way of life now characterised by sincerity and truth is now enjoined upon us. This becomes possible through the power of baptism and our incorporation into the Christian Passover.

With an economy of words but with consummate skill, John the Evangelist evokes the dawn hours and the atmosphere of that first Easter morning. Mary Magdalene on reaching the tomb found it empty. In haste, she summons Peter and the Beloved disciple who hurry to the tomb. We are not given any information as to their emotions or state of mind, and can only infer how they must have felt. The Evangelist adds the curious detail that the other disciple outran Peter on the way to the tomb. Was he therefore much younger? He reached the tomb first but did not enter. Again, may we surmise that this was out of deference to Peter? When the two apostles entered the tomb they found it empty and, intriguingly but without explanation, found the cloth which had covered the Lord's face placed separately by itself. The Evangelist remarks that the Beloved Disciple on witnessing the scene of the empty tomb now came to realise the truth foretold in the Scriptures of Israel that the Messiah would rise from the dead. It was only in the light of the empty tomb that the Scriptures now made sense. The story that was Easter morning made all the difference.

EASTER MONDAY

Readings: Acts 2:14, 22-33; Matthew 28:8-15

*Do not be afraid. But go and tell my brothers
that they are to leave for Galilee;
they will see me there.*
Matthew 28:10

The outpouring of the Holy Spirit at Pentecost is pre-
supposed in our reading from the Acts of the Apostles.
A transformed Peter addresses the Jerusalem crowd
and gives a powerful account of how God was at work
in the life, death and resurrection of Jesus of Nazareth.
The signs and miracles wrought by him during his public
ministry proved that God was with him, while the malice
and cruelty of his death on the cross, far from being
an accidental tragedy, happened in fact with God's
foreknowledge. God would not allow the deed of wicked
men to have the final say, and by his almighty power
released Jesus from the stranglehold of death and raised
him to life. As a proof that this was part of God's plan,
Peter cites a passage from Psalm 15 in which David
expresses his confidence that God would not allow his
body to experience the corruption of the grave. David has
died, Peter continues, and so his words were prophetic
and came to fulfilment when God raised Christ from
the dead. Of that there can be no doubt, Peter asserts,
for he and his fellow apostles were eye-witnesses to the

events they are now proclaiming. Christ, now enthroned in glory at God's right hand, has sent the promised Holy Spirit which explains the wonders surrounding this day of Pentecost.

The Evangelist Matthew relates the encounter of the risen Christ with the women and his words of reassurance that they are not to be afraid. Although in some sense Christ is different after his resurrection yet his relationship and ties of affection with his brothers remain. Far from forgetting them, the women are to tell his brothers that they are to meet him in Galilee. He wants to see them again and renew his friendship with them. The religious authorities, meanwhile, had been alerted to the rumours of Christ's resurrection and took steps to counteract them. The guards at the tomb were bribed to spread the story that the disciples had secretly stolen the body. What Matthew is implying here is that the startling truth of the resurrection is only accessible to those who have faith. Throughout his life of preaching and teaching Jesus met with hostility and disbelief, and his claim to enjoy a unique relationship with God ultimately led to his crucifixion. Those who so strongly opposed him in life would hardly be convinced that he had risen from the dead.

EASTER TUESDAY

Readings: Acts 2:36-41; John 20:11-18

I am ascending to my Father and your Father,
to my God and your God.
John 20:17

Peter's great Pentecost address concludes in Acts 2 with an appeal to his audience to repent of what they have done. In ringing words the Apostle declares that the person they crucified has now been exalted by God as Lord and Messiah. Jesus Christ is the one whom Israel awaited and hoped for, if only they knew it. And in a remarkable reversal of events, the crowd were moved by Peter's words and turned to the apostles for guidance and direction. In near sacramental language Peter states that their reconciliation with God involves three stages: be baptised in the name of Jesus Christ, have their sins forgiven, and so receive the gift of God's Holy Spirit. By accepting Jesus Christ as their saviour they are inheriting the promises God repeatedly made to Israel throughout its history. Peter's hearers were won over by the force of his arguments and a large number submitted to baptism that same day and became part of the first Christian community. The Church was growing already.

The carefully crafted scene of Mary Magdalene at the empty tomb is fully typical of the style of the Evangelist

John, both in its simplicity and theological depth. The inconsolable Mary seeks in vain the body of her Lord. "They have taken my Lord away", she cries, "and I do not know where they have put him." The Magdalene is unconsciously here uttering a profound truth. Jesus has now indeed been taken away, but has passed to the new and eternal life of the resurrection, a truth we can only apprehend through faith. Her persistence in the garden is amply rewarded when the risen Lord himself appears to her, although she mistakes him for the gardener. Only when he calls her by name does she recognise Christ. Here indeed was the Master she knew and loved, yet much had changed. Mary wanted to cling to the man Christ and never experience again the pain of losing him, but with his resurrection a new order had broken upon the world. Christ must now ascend to God his Father, and through him our mediator he would also be our God and Father. From now on Jesus Christ would be accessible to Mary Magdalene through faith alone, and as the first herald of the resurrection that was the good news she was to take to his brothers, and to us who believe.

EASTER WEDNESDAY

Readings: Acts 3:1-10; Luke 24:13-35

They told their story...
and how he was made known to them
in the breaking of bread.
Luke 24:35

As Luke gradually unfolds for us the history of the early Church in the Acts of the Apostles, he does so in the conviction that the power of the risen Christ is now active and at work in the preaching and ministry of the apostles. A simple story of an encounter between Peter and John with a crippled beggar makes the point dramatically. Peter is unable to meet the beggar's request for alms, but possesses what silver and gold cannot purchase, namely a share in that divine authority and power over sickness and evil which Christ himself exercised while on earth. Implicit in this healing miracle is the activity of the Holy Spirit which Christ promised to his disciples when he returned to his Father in heaven. Christ himself was endowed with the fullness of the Spirit at his baptism and since Pentecost Day that same Holy Spirit now resides in the Church. Christ's earthly ministry, far from ceasing with his death on the cross, now continues through the Church, and in a particular way through those who succeed the apostles in their office of proclaiming the gospel.

In his account of the two disciples on the road to Emmaus the Evangelist Luke has left us a rich and masterful resurrection story, highly instructive for the Church of every generation. As they walked along, Cleopas and his companion were reflecting on the tragic and disastrous event of Good Friday when their world seemed to collapse around them. The crucifixion of Jesus had put an end to their hopes and aspirations. The stranger who joined them on the way engaged in conversation with them and listened to their mournful account of what might have been where Jesus of Nazareth was concerned. Their sadness was compounded by rumours of his possible resurrection. At this point the unknown stranger chided them for their failure to understand their Scriptures in which all these things were foretold. The two disciples finally realised the identity of Jesus when he broke and shared bread with them; faith opened their eyes at this Eucharistic celebration but he had now vanished from their sight. Only afterwards did they realise the wonderful experience they had as Christ disclosed the meaning of the Scriptures to them. Luke has here given us a description of the Eucharist valid for all time. The Church will always discover the Lord Jesus afresh in the Scriptures and in the breaking of bread. He continues to speak to us and causes our hearts to burn within us as we share in that unique meal which we know as the Last Supper.

EASTER THURSDAY

Readings: Acts 3:11-26; Luke 24:35-48

Repent and turn to God,
so that your sins may be wiped clean.
Acts 3:19

The amazement of the crowd at the healing of the cripple provides Peter with the opportunity to expound the real reason for this miracle. In doing so, he sets before us the faith and conviction of the early Church in the person and identity of Jesus Christ, for it was by his power that the cripple can again walk. Peter recounts briefly the story of Jesus' betrayal and wrongful crucifixion and pins the blame firmly on those who had a part in it. But the God of their ancestors raised him from the dead and to this incredible fact Peter and his companions are witnesses. The Apostle continues his address with a conciliatory appeal to his hearers, excusing them for their ignorance resulting in Christ's death but which actually fulfilled the Scriptures that God's Christ must suffer. God is now offering them forgiveness of their sins and a new beginning if they will embrace him whom Moses and the prophets had long foretold. As Israelites it is to them that Christ has first come, proof that God has been faithful to his promises as written in the Scriptures. The long-awaited time of grace has arrived.

Following on the story of the encounter of the two disciples with the risen Lord on the road to Emmaus, Luke relates an appearance of Jesus to the Eleven and those with them. The full reality of the resurrection had not yet dawned on them and they were both frightened and confused at the apparition in their midst. Christ reassures them with his greeting of peace, and by showing them the marks of his wounds he proves that it is really himself they are seeing. By eating a meal with them he lays to rest their doubts as to the reality of his risen body. Yet again, as in the case of the two disciples on the road, the risen Christ opens up the Scriptures to them for it is there that they find the key to the mysterious events of the last few days which saw his arrest, suffering and crucifixion. The same Scriptures also foretold that he would return to life on the third day. He stands among them as the living evidence of the truth of what is written in Moses and the Prophets, as well as in the Psalms. Christ is here implying that it is he who fulfils God's plan and gives the definitive meaning to the Scriptures. This will be the gospel which the Apostles and those who come after them must proclaim to the very ends of the earth.

EASTER FRIDAY

Acts 4:1-12; John 21:1-14

It is the Lord!
John 21:7

The arrest of Peter and John for proclaiming the resurrection of Jesus reflects the treatment which Christ himself received at the hands of the authorities during his public ministry. Prominent in their arrest and imprisonment were the Sadducees who did not believe in the resurrection of the dead. The two apostles were put on trial before the highest ranking officials and required to give an explanation of their behaviour. Undoubtedly, Luke wishes us to contrast the courage and self-assurance of Peter here in the courtroom with his failings at the arrest and trial of Jesus. A new power was now operative in his life which caused such a transformation, that of the Holy Spirit. Peter was unflinching in his words and restated once more the essentials of the Christian faith. The man, Jesus from Nazareth, taken and put to death on a cross at their conniving, has been raised by God from the dead. He is alive and his power has been manifested in the healing of a cripple. In him alone is God's salvation to be found. Like a stone thought unfit for use by the builders, Jesus Christ has now become the foundation stone of a new building designed by God.

John the Evangelist offers us a carefully crafted and thought-provoking resurrection appearance of the Lord Jesus on the shore of Lake Tiberias on the Sea of Galilee. We are familiar with a similar lakeside story from Luke, 5:1-11. In John, Peter and a few of his companions spent the night fishing on the lake but caught nothing. In what is a feature of the resurrection narratives they did not know the stranger standing on the shore, but following his advice to try again they netted a huge catch of fish. The Beloved Disciple then recognised Jesus for who he was and this impelled Peter to make straight through the water to his Lord. This marvellous scene from the fourth Gospel is deeply and movingly symbolic. As the then Cardinal Joseph Ratzinger observed, we have here a picture of the Church in the morning of her life. There are Eucharistic overtones to the meal which Christ provided for his hungry disciples, and which he continues to provide for every generation of believers. And only by obeying the word and teaching of Christ will the Church succeed and be faithful to the task Christ gave to it. The human labours of Peter and the others were in vain without the presence of Christ. The large number of fish which did not tear apart the net is a sign of the unity of the Church which embraces all nations, yet is not torn asunder.

EASTER SATURDAY

Readings: Acts 4:13-21; Mark 16:9-15

*Judge before God whether it is right to obey you
or rather to obey God.*
Acts 4:19

Peter and John, here representative of the fortunes of the early Church, stand simple and uneducated but undaunted before the powerful and religious establishment of the day. They were recognised as belonging to the followers of Jesus. The presence of the healed cripple caused the Sanhedrin to pause and to admit that something wonderful had indeed taken place. Invoking their authority, they ordered Peter and John to refrain from speaking and preaching about the resurrection of Jesus. Such a command led Peter to declare that as a matter of conscience they must obey God before any human institution. After what they had witnessed and experienced in the drama of the death and resurrection of Jesus Christ, how could they possibly keep silent. They were eye-witnesses to unique events that would have significance for the whole world; no one or no power must prevent them from speaking about what God had accomplished in Christ. The theme of trial and persecution here depicted by Luke in the Acts stands as a prototype of what the Church would have to endure on her journey through history in her witness to the resurrection of Christ.

The gospel passage from Mark is typical of the style of this Evangelist, with post-resurrection episodes recounted with the minimum of words and detail. The theme of disbelief colours the three short encounters of the risen Christ with Mary Magdalene, the two disciples on the road, and the Eleven at table. Mary Magdalene's claim to have seen the Lord meets with incredulity, as did that of the two disciples travelling to Emmaus. The Lord himself took the Eleven to task for their failure to believe that he had risen from the dead. The truthfulness of the gospel resurrection stories underlines the awesome reality that was the resurrection of Christ, an occurrence that far surpassed normal human experience and one which could only be properly apprehended through faith and the assistance of the Holy Spirit. Equally brief is Christ's commission to the Eleven. They were to go out to the whole world and proclaim his gospel to everyone without exception. Through his resurrection all power had now been conferred on the glorified Christ. Although in his earthly ministry he did hint at a mission which would extend far beyond Palestine, as a rule Christ confined himself mainly to the 'House of Israel'. Now the word of life which is his gospel would know no bounds and the Church he founded was destined to be the Church of all nations.

SECOND SUNDAY OF EASTER – YEAR A

Readings: Acts 2:42-47; 1 Peter 1:3-9; John 20:19-31

Jesus stood in their midst and said,
'Peace be with you'.
John 20:21

In Acts, Luke presents a wonderful picture of the post-resurrection community, and in doing so has sketched a model for living for the Church of all time. The charter of the community was the teaching given by the apostles, the authoritative eye-witnesses to what Jesus said and did. The unity of mind and heart which existed characterised the community, nurtured and strengthened by the 'breaking of bread', a reference to the Eucharist, the table of the Lord's body and blood. It was also a community faithful to prayer and the praise of God. We see in this charming description outlines of what would become features of the universal Church: the Apostles' Creed, Unity, the Eucharist, and the Worship of God.

The First Letter of Peter has been written with the newly-baptised in mind, baptism being the believer's access into the mystery of Christ's resurrection. Peter speaks of God the Father bringing us to birth again and, unlike our first birth in this mortal life, this time we now have a sure hope because it is eternal and kept for us by God in heaven. The Apostle expresses himself aware that his readers are going through a difficult time because of their faith in Jesus whom they have never seen; but they are sustained by the joy which comes from that faith, and the knowledge that in the end they will receive the fullness of salvation.

On the first Easter evening the risen Christ appears among his disciples and, triumphant over the power of evil and death, greets them with his peace. His wounds are both marks of what he had suffered and proof that he really has risen from the dead. He empowers the apostles to continue the mission given to him by the Father, by sharing with them the spirit of his new life by breathing upon them. Jesus' act of conferring the Holy Spirit has been called the Johannine Pentecost. The apostles would also partake in his power to forgive sins, continuing his work of reconciliation in the world. By appearing to Thomas and dispelling his doubts as to whether he has truly risen from the dead, Jesus is addressing believers of every age. Thinking of the many, who would afterwards come to believe in him as the crucified and glorious Lord and saviour without ever seeing him, Jesus pronounced on them a blessing. Their faith is all the more meritorious for not having seen him.

Readings: Acts 4:32-35; 1 John 5:1-6; John 20:19-31

*The multitude of believers
were of one mind and one heart.*
Acts 4:32

The young Church in Jerusalem, according to Acts, was characterised by a remarkable sense of unity, described by Luke as being of one mind and one heart. This community spirit even extended as far as a common sharing of possessions and property, so that no believer was ever in want. The ideal of a common way of life was one that would later hold considerable appeal for founders of religious orders and congregations. The preaching of the apostles centred on the resurrection of the Lord Jesus, a ministry they carried out with great effectiveness and power. The transformation in the apostles and the courage with which they proclaimed the gospel is quite astonishing, and throughout Acts Luke will remind his readers that this is the work of the Holy Spirit.

The First Letter of John shares a common theological language with the Gospel of John. In his dialogue with Nicodemus (Jn 3) Jesus spoke about the necessity of re-birth before a person can enter the kingdom of heaven. A similar baptismal theme recurs in this passage: to believe in Jesus and so be baptised makes us children of God.

The writer underlines the ethical consequences of baptism which are to observe the commandments as Christ has given them to us. The baptised Christian can accomplish this through sharing in the victory over the world already gained by Christ, the Son of God (Jn 16:33). Christ was fully human and our redemption took place by the shedding of his blood. The deeper insight given by the Spirit of truth serves to strengthen and deepen our faith in the full reality of who Jesus really was.

[Gospel: see Second Sunday Year A, p.26]

Readings: Acts 5:12-16; Apocalypse 1:9-13,17-19;
John 20:19-31

*Many signs and wonders were accomplished
among the people through the hands of the apostles.*
Acts 5:12

In the Acts of the Apostles Luke constantly underlines
how the ministry of the apostles was a continuation and
extension of Christ's own ministry while on earth. The
gospels relate how Christ cured people afflicted with a
whole range of sicknesses, both spiritual and physical,
(e.g. Mk 6:56). Following his example Peter also heals
the sick and troubled in this short reading from Acts.
Luke is affirming that the work begun at the Incarnation
of Christ has not ceased with his Ascension and departure
from his disciples, but is now permanently embodied in
the community which he has left behind, the Church.
The same Holy Spirit who descended upon Jesus at his
baptism in the river Jordan, so equipping him for his
public ministry of healing and forgiving sins, now resides
in Peter and the other apostles. They too have been
invested with power and authority from on high.

In the book of the Apocalypse the visionary, John, has
been banished into exile on the Greek island of Patmos
because of his witness to Christ. A figure, like a Son

of Man, appears to him in a vision and orders him to commit to writing all that will be revealed to him. The aim of John's book, rich in its allusions and references to the Old Testament, will be to console and comfort those Church communities presently enduring persecution for their faith in Jesus. In striking language, Jesus announces that he is the one who holds the keys of death and the nether regions, meaning that he now has sovereignty and power over death and the prince of evil. As the once dead and now risen Lord, he is Lord of history and so can tell John to write down the account of present tribulations and what still remains to take place.

[Gospel: see Second Sunday Year A, p.26]

Readings: Acts 4:23-31; John 3:1-8

What is born of the flesh is flesh,
and what is born of the Spirit is spirit.
John 3:6

The reading from Acts depicts the early Church at prayer. Peter and John had returned unharmed from their trial at the hand of the authorities and the confident community of believers gave thanks and praise to God for the happy outcome. At the heart of their prayer lay the conviction that Jesus was indeed the anointed one of the Lord and recent happenings had served only to further God's plan as revealed in the Scriptures. The quotation from Psalm 2 is applied specifically to the fate of Jesus when the nations in the person of Herod and Pontius Pilate conspired and rose up against him. God foresaw their wicked deeds, and in his wisdom turned them into good. The crucifixion of Jesus Christ was no mere accident therefore, or just another sad chapter in human history. This first Christian community, with its faith rooted in the crucified and risen one, grew more and more in the awareness that they were the true heirs of the promises God made to Israel. Their appeal to God for courage and boldness in proclaiming the message in the face of ongoing adversity and persecution was answered by a further outpouring and experience of the promised Holy Spirit.

The Evangelist, John, records a visit of Nicodemus, a prominent Jew, to Jesus, with the clear intention to hear and learn from him. John remarks that he came 'by night', a possible symbolic allusion to Nicodemus' ignorance of spiritual matters and to Christ who is the light. The crass ignorance and misunderstanding of Nicodemus become evident as the dialogue with Jesus unfolds. He remains on the level of what Scripture calls 'the flesh', and his outlook is of this world. The truths which Christ came to reveal can be grasped only by someone who has undergone a spiritual rebirth and so perceives things from an entirely different perspective, a spiritual one. The language which Jesus uses to instruct Nicodemus, stressing the necessity to be born again through water and the Spirit, is the language of baptism and reflects the profound spiritual transformation which takes place through baptism. The words of Jesus in this passage would lay the foundation for the Church's belief in the necessity of baptism and the gift of the Holy Spirit to enable one to become a believer, and so penetrate the mysteries of the kingdom which Jesus came to proclaim. By employing the simile of the mysterious nature of the wind blowing where it pleases, the Lord is hinting at the ultimately mysterious workings of the Holy Spirit both in the lives of individuals and of the Church as a whole.

Readings: Acts 4:32-37; John 3:7-15

None of them was ever in need.
Acts 4:34

In Acts, Luke gives us a wonderful snapshot of the life and practice of the first believing community in Jerusalem under the guidance of the apostles. There was a common sharing of possessions and the needs of all were met. The proclamation of the faith centred on the resurrection of Jesus which the apostles preached with great power and conviction, gaining them widespread respect and favour among the people. The manner of life of these first Christians reflects the radical nature of Christ's own lifestyle and the demands that fidelity to his gospel entailed. The practical step of pooling all that they owned reflects the Lord's own attitude to material possessions during his public ministry, as well as being an expression of their love for one another which Christ insisted was to be the hallmark of his disciples. This particular passage from Acts has subsequently inspired many to follow the example of these earliest Christians by leading a life of simplicity, sharing and detachment from the things of this world. It made a deep impression, for example, on Augustine of Hippo (354-430), and he and his friends modelled their community life on it. This ideal of Christian living has lost nothing of its challenge.

In the gospel Jesus leads Nicodemus, the teacher in Israel, to an appreciation of higher things, to a deeper understanding of what is spiritual as opposed to what merely pertains to the outlook of the flesh and this world. John's Gospel here presents Jesus speaking to Nicodemus but the dialogue probably also reflects the apologetics of the early Church in its engagement with the synagogue and the Jewish religious leaders. Jesus, bearer of divine truth, can speak with authority of what he knows and has seen, but that witness is rejected by his own people. His teaching belongs to another order entirely because he himself ultimately comes from another world. Though not mentioned by name, the cross is implicitly alluded to here. As Son of Man, Jesus must be 'raised up', which is John's way of referring to the crucifixion of Jesus. The Evangelist never separates the cross and glory, for it will be through his death on the cross that Christ will be raised up to the glory of the Father. Scripture had already foreshadowed the cross when Moses erected on a pole the bronze serpent in the wilderness to save the afflicted Israelites (Num 21:4-9). So, Jesus declares, the one lifted up on the cross will bring salvation and healing to those who approach him in faith.

SECOND WEEK OF EASTER – WEDNESDAY

Readings: Acts 5:17-26; John 3:16-21

*God so loved the world
that he gave his only-begotten Son.*
John 3:16

Acts makes plain today that every human attempt to halt the progress of the gospel was destined to fail. Acting out of jealousy, the Sadducees had the apostles thrown into prison with the intention of arraigning them before the full Sanhedrin, the supreme ruling body in Israel. Yet the Word of God brought by Jesus will not be chained, as Paul would later remark, (2 Tim 2:9) and by divine intervention the apostles found themselves free. In the gospel resurrection narratives we are told the risen Lord was no longer bound by the limitations of time or space, and that very same risen power was evident in the manner of the apostles' release from the common prison. The proclamation of the new life won for the world by the cross and resurrection of Christ must not be thwarted by any human agency but must be heard by all in Jerusalem. The miraculous deliverance of the apostles from prison also underlines how Christ's victory on the cross has broken the stranglehold of wickedness and evil, and so we might say that the progress and spread of the gospel cannot but succeed.

The dialogue with Nicodemus reaches a climax with the sublime utterance of Jesus that such was the extent of God's love for the world that he gave his only Son, whose mission into the world was to be the bearer of God's salvation. Christ has come to save, not to condemn. A characteristic feature of the Fourth Gospel is John's insistence that those who refuse to accept the claims of Jesus as the one divinely sent have already passed judgement on themselves. In wilfully rejecting the claims of Christ such people have excluded themselves from the realm of God's love and truth. The Evangelist draws on the categories of light and darkness further to exemplify the drama which confronts human beings. A godless, unbelieving way of life is tantamount to preferring the darkness with all its sinister overtones. With the coming of Jesus the true light has entered the world, the light which gives fresh vision to the human race and gives access to the truth of God. The terms truth, light and life are all but interchangeable in John's Gospel. The actions of a person determine whether he remains under the power of darkness and so estranged from God, or whether he belongs to the kingdom of God's light brought to us by Christ.

Readings: Acts 5:27-33; John 3:31-36

We must obey God rather than men.
Acts 5:29

Peter and his fellow apostles are brought before the Sanhedrin to explain why they continue to preach the name of Jesus despite having been forbidden to do so. The presence of the apostles before the supreme ruling body of Israel mirrors the trial of Christ himself, and Luke is here underlining the fact that the followers of the Lord can only expect to be treated in the same way that he was. In response to the accusation that the Sanhedrin were being blamed for the death of Jesus, Peter unflinchingly asserts the truth of the resurrection from the dead of the one crucified on a tree, a powerful act wrought by God to give the world its saviour. Nonetheless, Almighty God has remained faithful to his people Israel, and through Jesus he now offers them the opportunity of repentance and the forgiveness of their sins. They were the first to receive the promises of God, and to Israel the news has now first come that these promises have been fulfilled in Jesus Christ. The apostles are indeed witnesses to all that has happened, and through the gift of God's Holy Spirit can explain the full meaning of these marvellous events. These claims served only to further enrage the members of the Sanhedrin and they even contemplated having the apostles put to death.

The role of John the Baptist in the Gospel of John is primarily one of giving witness to Jesus. The Baptist has no doubt as to his proper place in the divine scheme of things. He belongs to the earth and inevitably what he says pertains to this world. By contrast, the one who comes from above belongs to another and greater sphere and is consequently above all. He speaks only of what he has seen and heard in that other heavenly sphere, and as we know his witness was rejected by his own people, (Jn 1:11). When a person accepts the witness of Jesus he is thereby testifying to the truthfulness of God, for Jesus the Son speaks the words of God. He alone enjoys the fullness of the Holy Spirit and can speak with supreme authority. The unity existing between the Father and Son is such that Jesus acts with the full authority and permission of his Father. There can be no disharmony whatever between the Father and the Son. This complete unity between the Father and Jesus means that whoever refuses to believe in Jesus is estranged from God and alienated from the life of grace. In biblical language such a person falls under the wrath of God.

SECOND WEEK OF EASTER – FRIDAY

Readings: Acts 5:34-42; John 6:1-15

*They left the presence of the Sanhedrin rejoicing that
they were found worthy to suffer humiliation
for the sake of the name.*
Acts 5:41

While the Sanhedrin puzzled over what to do with the
apostles, a respected citizen and teacher of the Law,
Gamaliel, counselled prudence. Later in Acts (22:3),
we will meet the same Gamaliel as the teacher of Paul.
Citing the fate of two previous would-be leaders in Israel
who gathered bands of followers around them, Gamaliel
related how the aspirations of these two pretenders came
to nothing and they perished, while their followers were
scattered. Then raising the tone of his argument to a more
theological level, Gamaliel cautioned the members of the
Sanhedrin and urged them to have an open mind where
the apostles were concerned lest they find themselves
thwarting the plan of God. His intervention persuaded
them not to pass the death sentence on the apostles,
instead they were scourged and set free. The integrity and
courageous intervention of a good man at this important
juncture made an invaluable contribution to the progress
of the early Church. Note how the rough treatment of the
apostles at the hands of the Sanhedrin reflects in large
measure what Christ himself underwent in his passion.

Opposition and suffering served only to spur the disciples on, and their mission of proclaiming the gospel of Jesus Christ continued without interruption.

The extended chapter 6 of John's Gospel, which has at its heart Christ's discourse on the bread of life, opens with the feeding of the five thousand from the little boy's five loaves and two fish. The Evangelist notes that the Jewish Passover was near, an implicit reference possibly to the unleavened bread of the Passover meal and to the true bread which Jesus would give us through his own forthcoming Passover. The disciples were at a loss as to how such a multitude could be fed from a few loaves. In language which has Eucharistic overtones, and surely points ahead to the Last Supper, Jesus took the bread, gave thanks to God and distributed it. Everyone present had more than enough and there was even a surplus. The Evangelist simply records what took place and does not attempt to explain the wonder of what Christ did. For John the feeding of the five thousand was one more sign given by Jesus, inviting both the crowd and us to look beyond the visible wonder to its underlying meaning, and above all to the one who accomplished it. Jesus would later explain the real meaning of the sign, but the people, sensing perhaps that the Messiah of Israel was in their midst, wanted to acclaim him king there and then. But the political way was not the way of Jesus, and the reaction of the multitude was misguided. John remarks that Jesus ignored the temptation and went off to the hills by himself.

Readings: Acts 6:1-7; John 6:16-21

It is I, do not be afraid.
John 6:20

The increase in the number of believers brought its own internal problems for the early Christian community. Greek-speaking Jews complained that their widows were being neglected at the expense of those widows of Hebrew origin in the daily distribution of charity. The apostles realised that they could not carry out both this work and the principal task of proclaiming the word of God. But a problem provided the opportunity for innovation, and after discussion it was decided to choose and appoint seven men who would devote themselves to this particular service. These seven, the most prominent of whom was Stephen, are traditionally understood as being the first deacons in the history of the Church. In what we might understand as a service of ordination, the community presented the seven to the apostles who prayed over them and commissioned them through the laying on of hands. The position and authority of the apostles in the growing Church is noteworthy here. It is they who would authorise and approve new ministers in the service of the gospel, ensuring that everything was carried out in accordance with their understanding of the mind of Christ. That role of authorisation and ordination continues with their successors in the apostolic office, the bishops of the Church.

When he walked on the waters of the Sea of Galilee Christ gives a further sign or indication of his real identity. By coming to the disciples on the water as they struggled in heavy weather he is demonstrating his divine power over the forces of nature. The as yet incomplete faith of the disciples led them to panic at the sight, but Jesus reassured them, as he does so frequently in the course of his ministry, and calmed their fears. The language of John's Gospel is often allusive and the words of Jesus to the disciples in the boat, 'It is I', recall the self-designation of God to Moses at the burning bush, 'I am who I am' (Ex 3:14). Later in the same gospel, Jesus would declare that he and the Father are one (10:30). Such is the uniqueness of this unity between Father and Son that the words and deeds of Jesus are in complete harmony with the will of his Father. The presence of Jesus on earth is none other than the presence of God. The disciples of Jesus quickly find themselves at the shore, safe from danger. An abiding lesson for the Church of every age, especially in the storms of life, is the need to recall the lordship of Christ over creation and to entrust herself fully to him in faith. Then indeed will she know security.

THIRD SUNDAY OF EASTER – YEAR A

Readings: Acts 2:14,22-33; 1 Peter 1:17-21; Luke 24:13-35

*And they told their story of what happened on
the road, and how they recognised him at
the breaking of bread.*
Luke 24:35

After the extraordinary event of Pentecost Peter addresses the cosmopolitan crowd gathered in Jerusalem and proceeds to explain what has just happened. In doing so, the Apostle gives a summary of what the first Christians believed about Jesus. The miracles and signs which he worked showed that God was with him, while his betrayal and death on the cross were foreseen by God. Following the teaching of Jesus himself, the early community was concerned to prove that the life and death of Jesus fulfilled what was written about him in the Scriptures. The interpretation and argument from Psalm 16, that God's holy one would never experience the corruption of the grave, apply specifically to the burial and resurrection of Christ. Peter declares that Christ has now been raised from the dead and taken his place with the Father, and has sent the Holy Spirit promised by the prophets in the last age. This is the reason for the wonders which the crowd have just witnessed.

Peter exhorts his readers, in all likelihood newly-baptised, to be watchful in their manner of living, because our sojourn here on earth is one of exile from our true homeland. Invoking the image of the Paschal lamb which was required to be blameless for the Jewish Passover meal, Peter reminds them that the lamb whose blood has redeemed them was infinitely more precious than anything silver or gold could purchase. The Apostle goes on to profess the apostolic faith in the divine nature of Christ who was with God from eternity, before the creation of the world. His resurrection from the dead and enthronement in glory are the unshakeable foundation of the believer's faith and hope in God.

The resurrection narrative of the two disciples on the road to Emmaus represents biblical story-telling at its most compelling. As they make their way to the village on that first Easter evening, the disciples are downcast and dispirited about what had befallen their master on Calvary. They did not recognise Jesus in the stranger who joined them as they related their sad tale and the reason for their despondency. Rumours of his possible resurrection only aggravated their sad situation. As the conversation developed they came to see the sufferings and death of Christ in an entirely different light as the true meaning of the Scriptures was explained to them. Cleopas and his companion persuaded the stranger to join them for a meal, during which he took bread, blessed, broke and gave it to them. It was at that very moment, when he broke the bread, that the full realisation dawned on them of who the stranger really was – the Lord Jesus. By recounting his Easter story, Luke wishes the future Church to understand that the place of encounter with the risen Lord is now to be found in the Scriptures and in the breaking of bread – the Holy Eucharist.

Readings: Acts 3:13-15, 17-19; 1 John 2:1-5; Luke 24:35-48

We have an advocate with the Father,
Jesus Christ, the just one
1 John 2:1

The first generation of believers originally proclaimed the message of Christ to the Jewish people and their authorities as a matter of priority. This extract from a sermon of Peter in Acts is an example of how they approached their task. They declared that the message they preach does not represent a break with the religious traditions of Israel, for it was the God of their Fathers who sent Jesus and whom they rejected. He was unjustly put to death by Pontius Pilate, but God raised him from death and to that fact the apostles are witnesses. Peter accepts that what the people of Jerusalem did to Jesus took place out of ignorance, and helped fulfil the Scriptures which predicted that the Messiah had to suffer. God now offers them a time of grace and repentance, and the opportunity to have their sins wiped away.

In his First Letter, John reflects on the atonement wrought by Jesus and the practical consequences for believers which follow from it. It would be better if we did not sin, but should we do so we have a mediator with the Father, Jesus Christ. He is just and so can effect our reconciliation, and not only ours but that of the whole world as well. We recall here the words of John the Baptist in the Fourth Gospel when he pointed out Jesus as the Lamb of God who takes away the sins of the world (Jn 1:29). Having received the grace of reconciliation, the believer must now lead a life according to the truth by adhering to the commandments as taught by Christ. To do otherwise would be a travesty of the truth.

Luke, in common with the other Evangelists, describes the fear and uncertainty of the apostles and disciples when the newly-risen Lord stood in their midst. They were startled and could not believe the evidence of their eyes. His wounds were physical proof that it was him, further supported by his eating a meal before their eyes. Luke adds that their joy knew no bounds. Prior to his death, Jesus had warned them that what was written in the Scriptures about him must necessarily come to pass (Lk 18:31). He opens their minds to understand the Scriptures in a new light. His passion, death and resurrection which were in accord with the divine plan as written in the Scriptures, would be the source of forgiveness of sins for the whole world. It would be the task of the disciples to bring that good news to all nations.

THIRD SUNDAY OF EASTER – YEAR C

Readings: Acts 5:27-32,40-41; Apocalypse 5:11-14;
John 21:1-19

*By his own right hand God raised this man up as leader
and saviour, to give repentance to Israel
and the forgiveness of sins.*
Acts 5:30

Just as Christ was put on trial before the Sanhedrin, the
supreme ruling body of the Jews, during his passion, so
now the apostles also find themselves arraigned before
the same Council. In reply to the accusation that they
are attributing responsibility for the death of Jesus to the
Sanhedrin, Peter replies that he and his fellow apostles
must obey God and their conscience and speak the
truth of what they had seen and heard where Jesus was
concerned. He did indeed die a violent death upon the
cross, but they are witnesses to the fact that God raised
him from the dead to be leader and saviour of Israel. In
his name repentance and the forgiveness of sins are now
offered to Israel. The apostles went on their way, glad to
have been humiliated for the sake of Jesus.

John, the seer, gives a description of the worship taking
place in heaven before the throne of God and the Lamb.
The scene is one of triumph, celebrating the victory
of Christ over death. As Paschal Lamb he was once
sacrificed but now lives in glory, worthy of the acclaim of

the whole realm of creation, beginning with the angels and reaching to the lowest and remotest parts of the earth. All creatures praise and worship God and the Lamb once slain in the eternal heavenly liturgy. The unusual imagery of the elders and the animals is perhaps an apocalyptic representation of those who bear the prayers of the saints on earth to the throne of God. Our liturgical worship here on earth is related to that taking place in heaven.

The final chapter of John's Gospel describes a post-resurrection appearance of Jesus to his disciples by the Sea of Galilee, and has parallels with the story of the miraculous catch of fish in Luke (5:1-11). Peter and his fellow apostles had laboured all night to no avail, but at the word of the yet unrecognised Lord on the shore they tried again, this time with astonishing success. Gradually becoming aware that it was Christ, they came ashore and found that he had breakfast prepared for them. The lessons inculcated by the Evangelist in this episode are that the presence of the Lord and obedience to his word can transform for the Church the most hopeless of situations, and the breakfast he provided is a sign of how he continues to feed his Church, this time with the food of his own body and blood. The dialogue of Christ with Peter draws the scene to a close. With his threefold declaration of love for Jesus in the presence of the other apostles, Peter is making amends for his denials at the time of the Lord's passion and Christ then confirms him as the shepherd of his flock, entrusting them to his care. The Apostle Peter has been given a unique role in the risen Lord's provision for the people he has redeemed by his blood.

Readings: Acts 6:8-15; John 6:22-29

This is the work of God:
that you believe in the one he has sent.
John 6:29

The parallels between the trial of Jesus before the Sanhedrin and that of the deacon Stephen in Acts are close and deliberate. Luke intends his readers to see how the followers of Jesus suffered the same fate as the Master himself. The charges levelled against Stephen that he dared criticise Moses, tried to subvert the Law, and foretold the destruction of the Jerusalem Temple were of a piece with the charges brought against Jesus during his trial (Mt 26:59-61). During his public ministry Jesus constantly taught his disciples that his way of suffering and rejection would be theirs as well. And so it was with Stephen. Despite the false accusations brought against him, Stephen's eloquence and wisdom inspired by the Holy Spirit proved more powerful than the trumped up charges of the religious authorities, and they were unable to master him in argument. With good reason the Acts of the Apostles is often called the book of the Holy Spirit, for the guiding force throughout the life of the first community was the Holy Spirit promised by Jesus and now a reality in the life of Stephen.

The crowd were enthusiastic about Jesus since he fed them with the loaves and the fishes. They were keen to see him again, desirous to have more of the same food. But as Jesus tells them, they were seeking him for the wrong reasons. Their outlook was purely materialistic and tied to the level of the flesh. Raising the dialogue to a higher plane, the Lord urges them to devote their energies in search of a food that would not perish, but which would endure forever. This was an altogether different kind of food which he, the Son of Man, could give them for he has the full authority from God to do so. In a manner characteristic of John the Evangelist's style, they pursue the question of what kind of work God wants them to do in order to have this food of which Jesus speaks. The answer takes us to the heart of the theology of John's Gospel: in order to have this food which satisfies and endures, Jesus says that they must accept him as the one whom the Father has sent into the world. Throughout the Fourth Gospel Jesus appeals again and again to his audience to believe that he is the Messiah promised to Israel, spoken of by Moses and the prophets. The miracles he worked, which John calls signs, were not for their own sake, but were intended to lead to a deeper awareness of the person who accomplished them, he as the Son of the Father.

THIRD WEEK OF EASTER – TUESDAY

Readings: Acts 7:51-8,1; John 6:30-35

I am the bread of life.
John 6:35

The ever-growing bitterness and division between the followers of Jesus and the Jewish authorities reaches a climax with the drama of Stephen's trial and his subsequent death by stoning. Stephen accuses them of wilful hardness of heart, even to the point of resisting God's Holy Spirit by their actions. Their present arrogant behaviour merely follows the pattern of their ancestors who persecuted those very prophets who spoke of the coming of the Messiah, Jesus Christ. By having Jesus put to death they have betrayed the Law which God himself gave to them. Stephen concludes his long address by declaring that he sees heaven opened and has a vision of the divine glory, with the Son of Man at the favoured right hand of God. Here again is articulated the fundamental belief of the Jerusalem community, that Jesus the Son of Man lives now in the splendour of God's glory in heaven. Such a confession from Stephen in the divinity of Christ proved too much for his audience and in a manner akin to lynch law they stoned him to death. The final words of the first Christian martyr resemble closely in sentiment those of Christ as he hung dying on the cross. Just as Christ committed his spirit into his Father's hands, and prayed for forgiveness for his executioners (Lk 23:34,46), Luke portrays Stephen doing exactly the same. Saul, who will figure prominently in the later chapters of Acts, now makes his first appearance and entirely approves of Stephen's killing.

As the dialogue of Jesus with the crowd unfolds, they demand a sign from him before they will believe and invoke the story of the manna in the desert which Moses gave to their starving forefathers. In recalling the figure of Moses they are implicitly contrasting Jesus with the great Israelite lawgiver. Can he perform a similar feat? Jesus corrects their perception, for it is God himself, not Moses, who provides the true bread which comes from heaven and which is far superior to what Moses gives. In their eagerness to have this bread, and probably still thinking of the meal of the loaves by the Sea of Galilee, they ask Jesus to give it to them. His response was of a kind they were surely not expecting, for Jesus stated forthrightly that he himself was the true bread which gave life and which has come down from heaven. In his person he represents the food and drink which endures and ultimately satisfies. To partake of this food, a person must first come to Jesus, which means accepting his teaching and believing that he is the one who has come from God. Later in this same discourse Jesus will express this teaching on the bread of life in Eucharistic language, but initially he is referring to himself as the one whose teaching leads to true life because that teaching comes from God.

Readings: Acts 8:1-8; John 6:35-40

Those who were scattered proclaimed the
Good News of the Word.
Acts 8:4

The death of Stephen marked the beginning of a persecution of the Jerusalem Church, and Luke records that with the exception of the apostles the rest of the believers were forced to flee the city. The ominous figure of Saul of Tarsus is mentioned as one of those involved in the persecution and attempted suppression of the Church. However a consequence of their expulsion from Jerusalem was the spread of the faith to the surrounding areas, including the region of the Samaritans. The people of Samaria were traditionally at odds with the Jews and were held in contempt, and now by a strange turn of events they would be among the first foreigners to have the gospel of Christ preached to them. God's providence ensured that the death of Stephen and the flight of believers from the holy city, far from hindering the progress of the Word of Christ actually advanced it instead. The continuity between the earthly ministry of Christ and his preachers becomes evident in the work of Philip the deacon among the Samaritans. The miracles, or signs, which he wrought, especially his healings and exorcisms, showed that the kingdom of God first manifested in Jesus had now reached the Samaritans. Philip's mission there found fertile ground.

In our extract from John's Gospel Christ proclaims to the crowd that the nourishment he offers will not leave a person hungry or dissatisfied. But faith is necessary to avail of this food, and the complaint of Jesus is that he has yet to find that faith despite his visible presence among them. All who respond to the mystery of God's grace at work in their hearts will come to Christ and be welcomed by him. There can be no dichotomy between the work of the Father and that of Christ, for the Father has sent the Son precisely to carry out his will. That will or saving purpose of God embraces both this life and the life of the world to come, for Christ on earth is the source of God's salvation for everyone who comes to him and the guarantor of eternal life hereafter in the resurrection of the dead. Christ is insistent on the unity of will between the Father and himself: those who look upon the Son with the eye of faith have eternal life here and now through anticipation, and have Christ's own promise that he personally will raise them to life on the last day. The developed, sublime teaching enshrined in these verses, perfectly exemplifies the literary technique of the fourth Evangelist. In the dialogues of Christ with Nicodemus or the Samaritan woman, for example, (chapters 3 and 4), the conversation begins on a relatively simple level and gradually evolves into a teaching that is both theologically developed and profound, as is evident here in the so-called Bread of Life discourse.

Readings: Acts 8:26-40; John 6:44-51

*The bread which I shall give is my flesh
for the life of the world.*
John 6:51

The encounter of the deacon Philip with the Ethiopian is another sign of how the gospel of Jesus was spreading beyond the confines of Israel, and a hint of its ultimate universal destination. Luke is at pains to stress how this encounter was the work of the Spirit and so was divinely inspired. The royal official was clearly well disposed to the Jewish faith as he had been on pilgrimage to Jerusalem and was reading the prophet Isaiah as he returned home. The well-known passage from Isaiah formed part of the Suffering Servant Song (52:13-53:12), and the Ethiopian inquirer wondered as to the identity of the suffering one referred to by Isaiah. Philip proceeded there and then to evangelise him and explain the truth about Jesus, who was in fact the humble and maltreated servant spoken of in prophecy by Isaiah. The belief of the first Christians that Jesus was the one foretold by the prophets emerges clearly in this incident. The central importance of baptism from earliest times as the doorway into the life of the Church is also evident here, as Philip accedes to the eunuch's request and baptises him at a nearby pool. Luke concludes the episode by noting how Philip went on to preach the Good News of Jesus in different towns, with the implication that of its very nature the gospel was unstoppable.

The unity of purpose between God the Father and Jesus his Son is once more underlined in the Gospel of John. Such is the oneness between Jesus and God that anyone earnestly seeking the truth about God will necessarily come to Jesus. The quotation from Isaiah (54:13), foretelling the day when all will be taught by God directly, applies specifically now to Christ as the one who teaches, God's own Son. Respecting the Jewish tradition that God cannot be seen by any human being, Jesus asserts that there is one who has seen him and has come from God, meaning himself. Resuming again the theme of the manna, Jesus contrasts the fate of those long ago who ate the manna in the desert and are now dead. The bread that he will give brings life, as well as the pledge of future unending life. The food which Moses provided was of short and limited duration, while the bread which Jesus offers will endure for ever because its origin is in heaven. The reading ends by referring implicitly to the cost at which this bread is made available. In a direct reference to the Eucharist, Christ states that the bread he speaks of will be his own very flesh, given for the life of the world. By this he intends us to understand that through the sacrifice of himself on the cross he will become bread for the world.

Readings: Acts 9:1-20; John 6:52-59

Saul, Saul, why are you persecuting me?
Acts 9:4

A cardinal moment in the life of the early Church was the conversion of Saul of Tarsus, related in some detail by Luke in Acts. It would also prove in the longer term to be a major turning-point. As Paul himself tells us, (Phil 3: 5-7; Gal 1:14-15) he was a Pharisee whose zeal knew no bounds, and fanatical in his hostility towards the followers of Christ. The defining feature of Paul's conversion was the appearance to him of the risen Christ, who identified himself with his suffering disciples when he asked Paul why he was persecuting him. In his letters afterwards, Paul the missionary would teach that the Church is the Body of Christ, Christ the Head and we the members. The idea may well have originated through his conversion experience. The fearful disciples in Damascus needed divine reassurance before they would engage with and embrace their erstwhile tormentor. The Lord's words to Ananias outlined the new convert's future career as a 'vessel of election', to take Christ's name before nations, kings and the people of Israel. In a quite astonishing turn of events, we are told that the newly baptised Paul began to preach that the Jesus whom he once despised is in truth the Son of God. A fresh and decisive chapter had opened in the history of the Church.

In John's Gospel Jesus is often presented as a cause of dispute and division, and his words here referring to himself as the bread of life are no exception. Despite the objection of his hearers, the Lord refuses to tone down his elevated claims and goes on to deliver what the Church has always understood as strictly Eucharistic teaching. He speaks directly of the necessity of eating his body and drinking his blood in order to have access to the life he offers. Sharing in this unique food will bring a person into the most intimate communion with Christ, resulting in the mutual indwelling of two persons, Christ and the believer. That union is life-giving in the fullest and most profound sense because it has its roots in God. As the Son, Christ owes his whole life to his Father, so consequently the believer in Christ through partaking of this food, shares in the union of Father and Son. This extended discourse of Christ on the true bread from heaven means there can be no comparison with the manna in the desert which was purely transient and of this world, whereas the bread Christ gives is enduring and eternal.

Readings: Acts 9:31-42; John 6:60-69

It is the Spirit which gives life;
the flesh is of no avail.
John 6:63

In summary fashion, Luke indicates how the Church was reaching out from Jerusalem to Judea, Galilee and Samaria. There is a sense of quiet reassurance to his remark that this missionary expansion took place in a community characterised by the fear of the Lord and enjoying the consolation of the Holy Spirit. In these chapters of Acts, Luke is describing a pattern of the first years of the Church which would be valid for the Church throughout its future history: a story of progress through light and shadow. The tragedy of Stephen's death was somehow balanced by the wonder of Paul's conversion as the early community consolidated its faith in the Lord Jesus. Luke continues to underline how the power of the risen Christ remains an enduring force in the ministry of the apostles. Peter restores the crippled and paralysed Ananias to full health or rather, as Peter declares, Jesus Christ was in fact the real one responsible. Faith in the presence of the Lord at work in Peter prompted the believers in Jaffa to send for him when the devout and devoted Dorcas died. In a scene very reminiscent of Christ raising the official's daughter (Mk 5:40-41), Peter raises Dorcas to life and further bolsters the townsfolk's faith.

The sublime bread of life discourse ends with division among Jesus' audience and disciples. His uncompromising words on himself as the bread which has come down from heaven met with incomprehension. Christ remains unyielding and states that only those who have faith can grasp the full extent of his teaching. In his conversation with Nicodemus Jesus had stressed the necessity of moving beyond an outlook of the flesh to one which is governed by the Spirit, otherwise his words, which are words of life, will fall on deaf ears. That all-important dimension of faith was lacking here, and blame attached to those who resisted the impulse of the Father's promptings and so refused to listen to Jesus. Referring to his awareness of the one who would betray him, Jesus presents Judas as a symbol of those who have hardened their hearts and prefer to follow their own wilful ways. The Evangelist remarks laconically that many of his disciples no longer walked with Jesus, who now addresses the Twelve directly and pointedly: did they also wish to go away? Their spokesman, Peter, responded on their behalf with his magnificent confession of faith in Jesus, that he in truth spoke the words of God and that their faith in him as 'the holy One of God' remained unshaken. The Twelve, and the bishops who succeed them, will be the guardians of that same faith in Christ for all time to come.

Readings: Acts 2:14, 36-41; 1 Peter 2:20-25; John 10:1-10

Repent, and be baptised every one of you
in the name of Jesus Christ.
Acts 2:37

Peter's extensive Pentecost sermon closes with an appeal to the Jews assembled in Jerusalem to open their hearts in faith to embrace the one who was crucified, because by raising him from the dead God has given him the divine title of Lord and demonstrated that he is the Messiah. In response to their question as to what they should do, the Apostle urged them to repent, change their outlook, be baptised in Christ's name, and receive the gift of the Holy Spirit. These catechetical steps would become standard for all converts to the Christian faith. Peter stresses that Israel is a privileged race in God's sight and the promises that he has made good in Christ are intended first and foremost for them. They should seize the moment of grace now being offered to them through the apostles. Luke adds that Peter's preaching persuaded a large number to be baptised.

The passage from Peter's First Letter is an exhortation to those suffering for the Christian faith to endure their trials with patience. Christ is the supreme exemplar of innocent suffering, for by the wounds inflicted on him through his crucifixion he has brought us healing. The account of the Suffering Servant related in Isaiah (ch 53) provides the backdrop and the language of this text. Throughout the whole ordeal of his passion and death Christ raised no protest but committed himself totally into the hands of his heavenly Father. Peter reminds his readers that in their previous manner of life they resembled erring sheep, but now, thanks to their redeemer, they have returned to the safe and secure sheepfold of their true shepherd.

[Gospel: see Monday of Fourth Week, p.72]

FOURTH SUNDAY OF EASTER – YEAR B

Readings: Acts 4:8-12; 1 John 3:1-2; John 10:11-18

Dearly beloved, we are already the children of God,
but what we shall be has not yet been revealed.
1 John 3:2

Following their cure of a cripple (Acts 3), Peter and John are brought before the Jewish authorities and asked to give an explanation of what had just taken place. The outpouring of the Holy Spirit on Pentecost Day had transformed the apostles and Peter defended their behaviour with utter conviction, summarising neatly the essence of the Christian gospel. It was not they who had restored this cripple to health but the power of Jesus Christ active in their ministry. They had crucified him but God raised him to life, and applying the words of the Psalm to Jesus (118:22), the stone rejected by the builders has wondrously become the foundation stone. Jesus Christ, the crucified one, has now by God's plan and purpose become the Saviour of the whole world.

In a few sentences the First Letter of John describes our dignity as children of God and the future with God that awaits us in the life to come. This amazing dignity as God's children derives from our baptism in Christ, but has its ultimate roots in God's unbounded love for us. Since the world did not accept the Son of God it therefore refuses to acknowledge those who are his followers. The writer speaks of a future which at present remains hidden from us, but with the conviction of faith he knows that when it comes to pass we shall enjoy the vision of God and see him face to face. The apostle Paul expresses similar sentiments at the conclusion of his great hymn to love (1 Cor 13:12). In this present life we see dimly as in a mirror, but then we shall see God clearly, face to face.

Drawing on a much-loved pastoral image from the Scriptures of Israel, Jesus declares himself to be the true shepherd of his flock. In the Old Testament God was often portrayed as the shepherd of his people (e.g. Ezek 34); his Son, out of obedience to his Father, now assumes this role. Contrasting the behaviour of a hireling who has no real care for the sheep and flees when danger approaches, Jesus' concern for his flock is of an entirely different kind. A mutual intimacy exists between him and the sheep entrusted to him. Later, in the discourse after the Last Supper, Jesus speaks of a similar close relationship with his disciples under the figure of the vine and the branches (Jn 15). As the Good Shepherd, he will freely lay down his life in love for his sheep, and here he is alluding to his sacrifice on the cross which will become the source of sacramental life for the Church, above all in the Eucharistic food of his body and blood. His death on the cross as shepherd will also gather into unity the scattered peoples of the earth who do not yet know God, described as the sheep which do not belong to his fold.

FOURTH SUNDAY OF EASTER – YEAR C

Readings: Acts 13:14,43-52; Apocalypse 7:9,14-17;
John 10:27-30

In their conversaations with them, Paul and Barnabas
encouraged them to remain faithful to the grace of God.
Acts 13:43

[First Reading: see Saturday of Fourth Week, p.82]

After the cosmic dramas which have unfolded in the course of the book of the Apocalypse, which at base were the struggle between the forces of good and evil, and in which God's people and the Church have been caught up, John the seer gives us a description of a future which will be final and peaceful. At the centre of this description, rich in biblical allusions, is the new and heavenly Jerusalem, depicted as a bride arrayed to meet her husband. The prophets of Israel were fond of comparing the unique and intimate relationship of God to his people with that of a bridegroom to his bride. The bridegroom in this the new creation is Christ and the Church his bride. The ancient covenantal promises of God dwelling in the midst of his people will be fulfilled in that new order designed by God. The trials and tribulations endured by those whom the seer calls 'the saints' will belong to the past; and even death itself, the last enemy. Through the victory of Christ the victorious Lamb God will renew the whole of creation.

The departure of Judas from the Last Supper room sets in motion the hour of Jesus' passion. Whenever Jesus refers to his coming suffering and death in the Fourth Gospel he always uses the terms of glory and glorification. Judas has now gone to betray him, and for Jesus that means the beginning of his passage to glory. The cross and resurrection will be the means of revealing the full identity of Jesus as the Son of the Father, and the divine glory that he has enjoyed with the Father from eternity. In the revelation of the Son, the full glory of the Father will become manifest as well. The Great Commandment articulated by Jesus in the other gospels, that we must love God and our neighbour, finds expression here in the mutual love which must be a defining mark of his disciples. It is a love modelled on his love for them, and ultimately of the mutual love of the Father for his Son, in which the disciples are privileged to share.

Readings: Acts 11:1-18; John 10:1-10

*So God has even given the Gentile nations
the repentance that leads to life.*
Acts 11:18

A further and significant development for the life of the growing community was the baptism of the Centurion Cornelius and his household by Peter, presented in Acts as an initiative taken by God himself. Our passage today describes Peter's defence of his action. The Centurion was not Jewish, but clearly a good man and someone who feared God. He was instructed by an angel to send for Peter who would have something important to tell him. At the same time Peter had a vision from heaven of what traditionally were unclean animals in Jewish law, and despite his protests was ordered to kill and eat them. The vision, for emphasis, was repeated three times. While Peter was explaining the fundamental points of the Christian story about Jesus to Cornelius and those around him, to his surprise the Holy Spirit descended upon them and these Gentiles had what amounted to a Pentecostal experience. The Apostle, realising that God was sending a powerful message to him, immediately baptised Cornelius and his household. The horizons of the Jerusalem community were gradually being enlarged, and the baptism of Cornelius marked another decisive milestone on the road to the universal mission of the gospel to the Gentile world.

A major part of the tenth chapter of John's Gospel is taken up with the pastoral images of sheepfold, shepherd and sheep. In Old Testament times the Israelites spoke fondly of God as a shepherd, and these texts form the background to this chapter (e.g. Ezek 34). Later in this discourse (v. 14) Jesus will describe himself as the Good Shepherd. He begins by affirming that a true shepherd enters the sheepfold in the correct way through the gate, and not in any devious manner as a thief would do. He calls the sheep, and because they are familiar with his voice they confidently follow him to pasture. Should a stranger attempt to lead them, they would not acknowledge him. Jesus explains the meaning of the parable to his bemused listeners, and in language which underlines once more his claims that he alone is the source of God's salvation. He is the gateway to the life-giving pastures which God intends his people to have, for he alone has the true interests of his flock at heart. Those who enter the gateway through him will not be disappointed, and will find their deepest desires satisfied. The succession of other shepherds and rulers who preceded him pales by comparison. They sought their own interests rather than those of the sheep entrusted to their care, whereas the majestic words of Christ, that he came to bring life in abundance, sum up his entire mission on earth.

FOURTH WEEK OF EASTER – TUESDAY

Readings: Acts 11:19-26; John 10:22-30

For he was a good man,
full of the Holy Spirit and faith.
Acts 11:24

The death of Stephen proved unexpectedly to be the catalyst for the missionary thrust of the first Christians. Expelled from Jerusalem they took their faith ever further afield, as far as Phoenica and Cyprus. Luke however is at pains to stress that until now they confined their proclamation of the gospel to the Jewish people, though the borders were becoming blurred as they encountered Jews of Greek background and preached the Lord Jesus to them. The growing number of converts prompted the Jerusalem Church, being the Mother Church, to send a delegation led by Barnabas to assess the situation for themselves. The well-disposed Barnabas was pleased with what he found, and he urged the new believers to remain steadfast in their attachment to the Lord Jesus. Luke confers high praise on Barnabas by describing him as a good man and full of the Holy Spirit. Barnabas clearly played a key role in the life of the early Church, especially in the burgeoning community at Antioch where Paul and he spent a considerable time instructing and strengthening its members in the faith. We are told that it was at Antioch that the name Christian was first applied to followers of

Christ. Barnabas would subsequently accompany Paul on some of his missionary travels.

Jesus is surrounded by a hostile and menacing crowd in the Temple precincts who want him to state openly whether or not he is the Christ, the Anointed One of God, so earnestly looked for by Israel. He refuses to give a direct answer and challenges his hearers to examine with an open mind the many works he has accomplished in his public ministry. These miracles and healings bear witness to who he is, and he has wrought them with the full authority and power of God his Father, yet people still do not believe in him. Returning to the pastoral imagery of shepherd and sheep, Christ gives a deeper reason for the crowd's failure to believe in him. Their misguided assurance and confidence in the God of Israel, allied to their narrowness of outlook, prevents them from being open to the truth of what Jesus says and does. In his own words, they do not belong to his flock. The familiar refrain of the Fourth Gospel recurs again: the union of Christ with his Father is so intimate and inseparable that his work is perfectly in keeping with his Father's will, and can even be said to be the work of the Father. The sheep which he leads to the pasture of eternal life, those who believe and accept his claims, have been placed into his hands by the Father who will not allow the work of his Shepherd-Son to perish. What Jesus is spelling out to his audience here, is that believing in God necessarily entails believing also in him, his Son.

Readings: Acts 12:24–13:5; John 12:44-50

I, the light, have come into the world.
John 12:46

The understanding and spread of the word of God continued unchecked, and prominent among those responsible for this expansion were Barnabas, Paul and John Mark. For Luke the word of God in Acts means the whole Christian proclamation of Jesus as the crucified Lord and Christ. A short summary of those who were prophets and teachers in Antioch indicates how the Church there had assumed structures which clearly enjoyed the approval of the Apostolic Church in Jerusalem (12:25). The believers in Antioch were conscious of the inherently missionary nature of the message of Christ, and at a solemn liturgical gathering, marked by prayer and fasting, and under the guidance of the Holy Spirit, they designated Paul and Barnabas to embark on a missionary journey. This commissioning was formalised by the laying on of hands, a gesture already employed in the case of the seven deacons (Acts 6:6). The impulse for this wider outreach of the gospel came from the Holy Spirit, a constant theme of Luke, though initially the activity of Paul and his companions was conducted solely in the Jewish synagogues. The important part played by the synagogue in the spread of the Christian faith throughout the Greek-speaking world should not be underestimated.

The gospel passage from John has a poignant ring to it, because it represents Jesus' last public appeal to the Jewish authorities to believe in him as the one sent by God to Israel. After this he withdraws from the public sphere and confines his teaching to his disciples. Jesus repeats that to accept him is to act in accordance with the will of God. The Jewish people looked upon their Law as being a light, but with Jesus a greater light has now come into the world in order to dispel the darkness and error to which humanity is prone. His words and teaching are not ordinary but have a special character to them, for God himself is their source. Anyone who deliberately ignores and disregards this teaching and the one who propounds it will have no excuse on judgement day. God is speaking through his Son and is offering life to the world. The tragedy of the Fourth Gospel is that Jesus' audience appear unable to break out of their particular mindset and be open to the possibility that the God of their Fathers is now revealing himself once more in their history, and that the one spoken of by Moses and the prophets now stands in their midst. They failed to appreciate that God is sovereign and infinite and works in unexpected ways. Jesus Christ is the living expression of God's will, the Word made flesh (Jn 1:14), but their lack of faith prevented them from accepting this.

Readings: Acts 13:13-25; John 13:16-20

Truly, truly, I tell you,
the servant is not greater than his Lord,
or the messenger superior to the one who sent him.
John 13:16

Paul now travels to Psidian Antioch and there in the synagogue addresses the Jews and those who were associated with them, whom Scripture calls God-fearers. This is the first of three major discourses Paul gives in Acts, the others being to the Athenians and the elders of the Church of Ephesus (Acts 17 and 20). Paul starts his address by giving a rapid outline of the history of Israel, from the captivity and deliverance from Egypt, the desert wanderings, and the conquest and possession of the land of Canaan. Eventually there came the kingship of Saul, whom God displaced in favour of his chosen one, David. It was from the seed of David, Paul continues, that God has raised up the saviour he promised, Jesus. John the Baptist was the precursor of the saviour and prepared the way for his coming by summoning the people of Israel to repentance. In language reminiscent of the gospels John declares unequivocally that he is not the awaited Messiah, for such a title properly belongs to the one who follows him. Paul's speech here may be seen as an example of how the very early Church sought to present the Christian gospel to the Jewish people. The catechesis draws exclusively on the history of Israel and presents Jesus as the fulfilment of that sacred history.

Jesus has just washed the feet of his disciples in the Upper Room and this astounding act of humility sets the tone for his remarks on the consequences of discipleship. What the Lord says about status and service here in John is echoed throughout the other gospels. To have a part with him means imitating his ministry of service. They will have his authority as they go out to face the world, but they must not expect to be treated any differently than he has been. In a rare occurrence of the word in John's Gospel, Jesus tells his disciples that if they share his humble outlook they will indeed inherit a blessing from God. The gathering for the Last Supper was an intimate affair between Jesus and his chosen company of the Twelve, yet he was fully aware that it was overshadowed by the impending treachery of one of that number, Judas Iscariot. The quotation from Psalm 41 about the betrayal by a fellow guest at table highlights again how the fate of Jesus was foretold in the Scriptures, and that his destiny was to fulfil the divine plan contained in these same Scriptures. The foreknowledge of Jesus allows him to alert the other apostles to the forthcoming deed of Judas. The passage concludes with the assurance of Christ to his disciples that whoever welcomes them in his name will in fact be welcoming them as his messengers, with authority from God himself.

FOURTH WEEK OF EASTER – FRIDAY

Readings: Acts 13:26-33; John 14:1-6

You are my Son, today I have begotten you.
Acts 13:33

By addressing them as the children of Abraham, Paul is taking his hearers in the synagogue back to the roots of their faith. In accordance with the promises made by God to Abraham the message of salvation in Christ is now first proclaimed to them. The Apostle presents a very condensed catechesis of the Christian faith which would later become the basis of our Creed. Through ignorance of the true meaning of the prophets which they heard every Sabbath, the authorities and populace of Jerusalem unwittingly fulfilled what the prophets had foretold. They had Jesus innocently put to death by crucifixion under Pilate and then laid him in a tomb, all of which was in accordance with the Scriptures. But God raised Christ from the dead and his disciples are the witnesses to this very fact before the people, for they have seen him in his risen state. The good news which Paul brings is that the promises made to Abraham and to their ancestors have now come to pass. By raising his Son Jesus, the God of their fathers has made good his promises. Paul then quotes a verse from the second Psalm which the early Church understood as being particularly applicable to the resurrection of Jesus, who in a glorious and fully manifest way became the divine Son of the Father by rising from the dead.

Chapter 14 of John's Gospel begins what has been called the farewell discourse of Jesus to his disciples. The final words of Jesus to his chosen friends are personal and intimate, and are imbued with a rich Christological teaching. They also have as their purpose the preparation of the disciples for a future when Jesus is no longer physically present with them. Jesus in this passage tells his disciples that they are not to be unduly troubled at his departure. He has their true interests at heart and will have a place ready for them when he one day returns to gather them into his Father's house. Whereas the other Evangelists speak of Christ's second coming as one of judgement (e.g. Mt 25:31-46), the emphasis here is on Christ's return to bring his disciples home. They are puzzled by his remarks, and the question of Thomas provides Christ with the occasion to describe his life and mission in a language which on the surface is simple, but profound in meaning. The way to God now lies through him. The man Jesus Christ as the Son of the Father, and ever 'in the bosom of the Father' (Jn 1:18), can alone teach the world the truth from God and the truth about God. The path which leads to true wisdom here and to unending life hereafter lies through the Son, for to him the Father has handed over everything.

FOURTH WEEK OF EASTER – SATURDAY

Readings: Acts 13:44-52; John 14:7-14

When they heard this the Gentiles rejoiced and gave praise for the Lord's message.
Acts 13:48

The strenuous efforts of Paul and Barnabas to win over the Jewish authorities in Antioch of Psidia met with little success. Even the townspeople were maliciously prompted to turn against the Apostles, an action which made Paul realise that the rejection of his message by the Jewish authorities now opened the way for the admission of the Gentiles into the Church. Paul saw the design of God at work in these unpromising circumstances and his quotation from one of the Servant Songs of Isaiah (49:6) confirms this. The word of Christ, largely rejected by Israel, from now on would be unfettered and proclaimed to every nation on earth. The proclamation of Jesus Christ the Messiah first began in Jerusalem, then because of persecution and the consequent displacement from the city, gradually shifted to neighbouring regions. The truth however was gradually dawning on the early Church that because of the constant rejection on the part of the Jewish authorities the truth of the Christian message had, according to Scripture, to embrace the whole pagan world. Luke notes how delighted the pagans were to hear the gospel and be included in God's saving plan of salvation. The expulsion of Paul and Barnabas from the town led them to heed the advice of the earthly Jesus and shake the dust from their feet (Lk 9:5). In the joy of the Holy Spirit they were now free to engage in a much wider and greater mission with no boundaries.

The Evangelist John in his presentation of Jesus' teaching in this passage employs his familiar technique of dialogue, which with its conversational structure allows Christ to lead his disciples to a deeper understanding of his words. The perfect union of Christ with his Father both in word and in works forms the subject of our gospel extract. Having spoken at such length in his discourses about his Father, the disciple Philip asks Jesus that he may see the Father. Often in this gospel Jesus does not appear to answer a question directly, with the clear purpose of leading his interlocutor to a higher theological level. The Son may not be separated from the Father in any sense, and the life and work of Jesus in every detail is in complete conformity to the Father's will. In that sense to know the Son is also to know the Father. The God of Israel now reveals himself no longer through the Scriptures but in his incarnate Son. We might say that the face of Jesus is in truth the face of God. The indis-soluble nature of this oneness between Jesus and the Father would prove fundamental to the later Church's doctrine of the Holy Trinity. The passage concludes with the reference of Jesus to his intercessory role with the

Father, through which his disciples will achieve many wonderful things. His earthly ministry was confined to Palestine, now through his coming glory in the resurrection and favoured place at God's right hand their accomplishments in his name will reach the ends of the earth.

FIFTH SUNDAY OF EASTER – YEAR A

Readings: Acts 6:1-7; 1 Peter 2:4-9; John 14:1-12

Do not let your hearts be troubled.
John 14:1

[First Reading: see Saturday of Second Week, p.43]

In a striking description of the real and fundamentally spiritual nature of the Church, the apostle Peter describes the newly-baptised as constituting living stones in a temple which rests on the one cornerstone, Jesus Christ. The magnificent building of the Jerusalem Temple with its ritual and sacrifice has now been replaced with a religious reality of another order, no longer tied to a single city, one constructed by God and built on Christ. Peter quotes passages from the prophet Isaiah and Psalm 118 to show how the rejection of Christ and the establishment of this new temple had been foretold in Scripture, and therefore formed part of God's saving plan for the Gentile world. The Apostle concludes, in climactic fashion, with a description of the exalted dignity conferred by God on those belonging to the Church. They share the privilege once accorded to Israel of being God's chosen people.

In the intimate setting of the Last Supper Room Jesus prepares his disciples for his imminent withdrawal from them. His parting words are marked by a deep humanity and affection. He speaks as a teacher to his disciples, but also as a friend to friends. Assuring them that they will be forever in his thoughts, he is going to prepare a home for them with his Father. In the spirit of true friendship he wants them to be part of his company there. Jesus takes and answers the questions they put to him, while at the same time deepening their understanding of his identity and unity with the Father. As the Son he has ushered in a new dispensation, for the way to God is now to be found through him alone. The wholly singular nature of the relationship between himself and God his Father means that the words he uttered and the deeds he performed in the course of his public ministry can properly be said to be those of his Father. The relationship with his Father which Christ here expresses in simple language would later be described in Church doctrine more technically as the 'hypostatic union'.

FIFTH SUNDAY OF EASTER – YEAR B

Readings: Acts 9:26-31; 1 John 3:18-24; John 15:1-8

We know that he lives in us
by the Spirit he has given to us.
1 John 3:24

Not only did Paul encounter stiff opposition and hostility from his own Jewish people because he preached that Jesus was the Christ, but he also had to convince the believers in Jerusalem that his conversion was genuine. They were amazed that the once relentless persecutor of the followers of Christ could now be proclaiming him as Lord and Saviour. In his letter to the Galatians Paul himself refers to their astonishment (Gal 1:23). Barnabas played an important part in the early career of Paul and helped smooth the way for his acceptance in the Christian community. As we can see from his letters and the Acts, Paul was a fearless preacher of the gospel and on more than one occasion was in danger of his life from those who opposed him. To ensure his safety, the Church in Jerusalem sent him back to his own city of Tarsus.

A constant theme pervading the First Letter of John is that of mutual love, but a love which must be genuine and expressed in good deeds. Then our conscience, the inner sanctuary of our hearts, will not trouble us before God. At peace with ourselves, we can be at peace in his presence.

In John's view, the essence of God's commandments can be summarised by believing in the name of Jesus Christ and loving our neighbour. The touchstone of our faith is the divine sonship of Christ, whose name is above every other name, and who therefore teaches with supreme authority the commandment of love. Both the Gospel of John and the First Letter share the same conviction that faithful observance of the teaching of Jesus brings the believer into that circle of divine love which binds the Father and Son, and ultimately has its roots in their mutual gift of the Holy Spirit.

[Gospel: see Wednesday of Fifth Week, p.95]

FIFTH SUNDAY OF EASTER – YEAR C

Readings: Acts 14:21-27; Apocalypse 21:1-5; John 13:31-35

And the One sitting on the throne said,
'Behold I am making all things new.'
Apocalypse 21:5

[First Reading: see Tuesday of Fifth Week, p.93]

When the struggle between God's people and the evil forces led by the Devil have ceased and the victory finally gained, John the visionary gives us a picture of a transformed world, what he calls a new heaven and a new earth. The focus of that new creation will be a radiant and wholly purified Jerusalem, the city so often at the heart of God's dealings with Israel throughout her history. In the favoured language of the great prophets, Jerusalem will be adorned with all the beauty of a bride on her wedding day, and we can understand the city here as a symbol of the saints in glory before the throne of God. The ancient covenantal promise that God would come and dwell among his people is here realised, and the pain, suffering and tears which so often mark and deform human history will no longer exist. In marvellous words, we hear that the Lord God, the One sitting on the throne is going to refashion the whole of creation.

The treachery of Judas has set in motion the hour of Jesus' glorification. The Evangelist John has his own unique understanding of the passion and death of Jesus and presents them as the prelude or means to his glory with the Father. In the course of his gospel rather than allude directly to the cross of Jesus he speaks of him as being 'raised up' (Jn 3:14; 8:28). By his humble and sacrificial death on the cross Jesus is acknowledging the will of the Father as the supreme rule in his life, and so gives glory to God. In turn, the Father will glorify the Son by raising him from the dead and so manifest his divine and glorious nature to the world. What must characterise his disciples once he has gone is the mutual love they have for one another. Such love is much more than altruism or mere human feeling, but draws its strength and example from the love which Jesus has for them. Mutual love, charity, is the consistent thread common to all the New Testament writers. As Jesus' parting legacy, it remains the standard by which the Church must always measure itself.

Readings: Acts 14:5-18; John 14:21-26

*The Paraclete, the Holy Spirit, whom the Father will
send in my name will teach you everything.*
John 14:26

The violent attempts on the life of Paul and Barnabas
by those Jews and pagans who refused to listen to
them only served to facilitate the spread of the gospel
message in other towns of Lycaonia. By recording the
healing of a cripple by Paul, Luke the author of Acts is
keen to underline the continuity between the ministry of
Paul and the earthly healing ministry of Christ. Luke is
yet again making the fundamental ecclesiological point
that the risen Christ remains active with all his power
in the preaching and work of those he has called to
proclaim his gospel. The wild scenes which followed
this miraculous deed of Paul led the crowd to see in the
apostles living incarnations of two Greek gods. Such a
claim was abhorrent to Paul, but it did provide him with
the opportunity to speak to the local people about God
in terms which they would understand. In an example of
early Jewish-Christian preaching to Gentiles, the Apostle
urged them to turn away from the vain and empty
deities they worshipped to the living God whom he was
proclaiming to them. Paul offers the people of Lycaonia
natural grounds for believing in a God who created the

world, left traces of himself in creation, and cares for their material needs. In his great address to the Athenians, Paul would further attempt to speak to his audience in a manner compatible with their own religious outlook.

When the Lord speaks of love to his disciples he means a love that expresses itself in practical deeds, in the observance of his commandments. Such a love for Christ necessarily brings a person into the ambit of his Father's love. In response to a question from one of the Twelve, Jesus explains that faithful observance of his teaching will result in the indwelling of the Father and the Son in the believer. The Old Testament language of the covenant is reflected in these words of Jesus, when the prophets promised that God would come personally to dwell among his people (e.g. Ezek 37:27). That promise of Scripture becomes a reality in the Church through the death and resurrection of Christ and the incorporation of believers through baptism into the new risen life of the Son of God, a life that is necessarily a union also with God the Father. The full implications of Christ's teaching could hardly be grasped by the disciples in the Upper Room, and Jesus introduces the subject of the Paraclete or Comforter, the Holy Spirit, who will gradually lead them to a fuller understanding of all that he has taught them. The work of proclaiming Jesus as saviour and the mission of the Church can only properly begin with the outpouring of the Holy Spirit.

FIFTH WEEK OF EASTER – TUESDAY

Readings: Acts 14:19-28; John 14:27-31

*We must undergo many trials before we can enter
the kingdom of God.*
Acts 14:22

On this, his first missionary journey, the opposition to
Paul's proclamation of Christ as Saviour intensified,
and by being stoned he shared the same punishment
as Stephen. Undaunted, he did recover and continued
his missionary work. The passage of Acts indicates the
difficulties encountered by the early Church communities
established by Paul. These fledgling Christians need both
encouragement as well as permanent Church structures
in order to survive in an often hostile environment. Paul
saw as his task the implanting of the Christian faith,
and its embodiment in structures of ministry and church
elders which would enable it to grow with a strong sense
of identity. With their return to Antioch, where they
had been originally empowered for mission, Paul and
Barnabas had now completed their work. In Acts Luke
quotes the striking phrase that 'God had opened the door
of faith to the Gentiles'. Among the many wonderful
things the two apostles had to report was the increasing
influx of pagan converts who had no knowledge of
the Jewish faith. Paul's experience on his travels had
convinced him of the necessity of bringing the gospel of

the risen Lord to everyone without exception. This he believed was in complete conformity with the plan of God as revealed in the Scriptures of Israel.

The parting words of Jesus to his disciples speak of peace and reassurance. The uncertain peace and security so characteristic of this world are not what he offers them, but rather a peace and contentment of mind which he alone can give. The disciples can therefore face the future with confidence and equanimity. If they knew the full truth, the departure he speaks of would be a source of joy to them because he is returning to the Father, from where he would send the Holy Spirit. Speaking from the condition of his humanity Jesus acknowledges that the Father is greater than he, but in his glorious risen state he will be equal to the Father. The disciples are urged to accept this in faith now, but later in the period following Easter they will come to know the truth of his words. Christ's mention of the coming of the prince of this world shows how aware he is of his approaching passion and death, and of his imminent struggle with the power of death and evil. As Son of God, however, that same prince can exercise no power over him. As he prepares for his final hour Jesus states that he embraces it out of obedience to his Father. He is repeating here in different language the sublime sentiments he had expressed earlier to Nicodemus: *God so loved the world that he gave his only-begotten Son* (Jn 3:16).

Readings: Acts 15:1-6; John 15:1-8

I am the true vine,
and my Father is the vinedresser.
John 15:1

The reception into the faith of such a large number of non-Jewish converts gave rise to the first major crisis within the young Church. A serious division of opinion arose when those Christians who were once Pharisees travelled down from Jerusalem to Antioch and insisted that all new converts to the Christian faith in order to be saved must undergo circumcision and observe in all its detail the Law of Moses. This attitude caused much questioning in Antioch, and it was decided to send Paul and Barnabas to Jerusalem to seek advice from the apostles and elders there. On their way Paul and his companions encountered only joy when they related to the various communities the wonders God had worked through the pagans.

In Acts Luke relates in an almost factual way what amounted to a crossroads for the Church. A measure of the heat and depth of argument surrounding the Jewish-Gentile question can be gauged from Paul's account in chapter 2 of Galatians. The crux of the matter was whether the Church was to remain tied to Jewish religious and cultic observances which far from being necessary for salvation were deemed non-essential, or instead be a place of welcome for all people of any background who had faith in Jesus Christ. The arrival at a solution necessitated the convening of the first Ecumenical Council of the Church which took place in Jerusalem.

Christ now introduces the theme of the vine and the branches into his farewell discourse to his disciples. The figure of the vine was a well-known image for the people of Israel in the Old Testament (Isa 5:1-7), an image which Jesus now applies to himself. The disciples and the future Church will draw life from him, provided that they remain united to him. As ever in John's Gospel, Jesus does not act independently of his Father. Both Father and Son are one in the work of redemption, vividly expressed in the depiction of the Father as the vinedresser tending the vine which is his Son. The teaching of Christ in the Upper Room has a definite reference to the future and can be seen as a missionary mandate. The disciples are to go out into the world and labour in the vineyard of Christ. He expects their labours to be abundantly fruitful, but the condition for this fruitfulness depends on their adherence and fidelity to all he has taught them. Christ may be understood here as speaking directly to the historical Church of every generation in his parable of the vine and the branches. He alone remains the source of her life and energy; to depart from that source will lead to barrenness and failure. Moreover, the Church as the Father's favoured creation gives glory to God by the rich and fruitful lives of believers: *'It is to the glory of my Father that you should bear much fruit.'*

FIFTH WEEK OF EASTER – THURSDAY

Readings: Acts 15:7-21; John 15:9-11

God has made no difference between them and us,
having purified their hearts by faith.
Acts 15:9

The long-simmering dispute in the early Church over the Jewish-Gentile question was finally settled by apostolic authority at the Council of Jerusalem. Peter and James played a prominent role in the decisions arrived at. Speaking out of his own missionary experience, Peter stated that God had shown no distinction between Jew and Gentile by pouring the same Holy Spirit on the Gentiles as he did on them. The divine will was for all to believe in the gospel of Jesus Christ. In words replete both with compassion and common sense, Peter declares that laws should not be imposed on new Gentile converts which the Jewish people themselves were unable to observe. God's way for everyone now was the way of faith in the Lord Jesus. When Paul and Barnabas gave an account of their missionary work among those of pagan background, the leader of the Jerusalem Church, James, supported the position of Peter by quoting a text from the prophet Amos. Through his prophet almighty God had foretold that one day the nations would form part of his people. James drew proceedings to a close by stipulating that only the minimal number of obligations were to be laid on new converts from paganism. The unity of minds and the decision arrived at in Jerusalem meant that the Church could now freely embrace her world-wide mission to both Jew and Gentile.

The love which Jesus has known as the Father's Son is the same love with which he now encircles his disciples. That love is freely given, and it would later be understood by the apostle Paul in a very personal way as the Holy Spirit (Rom 5:5), the loving bond which unites the Father and the Son. For the disciples, however, that love must not remain purely theoretical but has ethical implications. The teaching of Jesus, which he calls commandments, must find practical expression in their manner of living. John presents Jesus here as the new Moses, bringing the law of mutual love. The true disciple must model themselves on the example of Christ himself whose whole life was one of obedience to his Father's will and command. By his faithful obedience Jesus remained fully within the sphere of his Father's love. The faithful disciple will likewise enjoy the protection of Christ's love. The passage ends on a note of joy. Christ does not intend his commandments to be a burden; rather, fidelity to them will bring his disciples abundant participation in that joy which is his as the Lord of life and death.

FIFTH WEEK OF EASTER – FRIDAY

Readings: Acts 15:22-31; John 15:12-17

On reading the letter, the community were delighted
at the encouragement it gave them.
Acts 15:31

The apostles and elders in Jerusalem, having reached unanimous agreement on the conditions for admitting converts of non-Jewish background to the Christian faith, sent a letter by a delegation headed by Paul to the Church in Antioch and elsewhere informing these communities of their decision. Even at this early stage in the history of the Church the role of the apostles was felt to be crucial where matters of doctrine were concerned, and the respect which Paul and Barnabas enjoyed in the eyes of the Jerusalem authorities is evident from the letter. The requirements for pagan converts laid down in this apostolic letter seem to be of a general religious nature, but would have helped soothed the sensitivities of the Jerusalem Christians for whom the Mosaic Law still retained much of its authority. The Church in Antioch welcomed the letter with relief and drew great encouragement from it. The outcome was that the Gentiles now enjoyed equal standing with Jewish converts within the wider Church. A major turning-point had been reached and as a result a new and highly significant era for the Christian faith, and for the world, had begun.

The Lord in the gospel explains further to his disciples the kind of love of which he speaks. It is a love modelled on his own utterly sacrificial love which he is about to demonstrate by giving himself up to death for the salvation of the world, here narrowed in focus and referred to as love for his friends. Christian love therefore can have no limits. The relationship of the disciples to Christ is no longer one of servant and Master but rests now on an entirely new level, that of friendship. Christ has let his disciples into those secrets which he alone can disclose and which later theology would call Revelation. As a true friend, the Son of God has communicated to them throughout his earthly ministry whatever he has learned from God his Father. He reminds his disciples that his choice of them was his initiative and through no merit of their own, what we would come to know as the mystery of divine grace. Christ's words are directed to the whole Christian Church and refer to the gratuitous and mysterious nature of the call to baptism and the gift of the Christian faith. Returning to the theme of fruitfulness, Christ will expect a rich harvest from the life and witness of his disciples. He adds that his role as mediator with his Father will ensure that they, and by extension the wider Church, will lack nothing for their mission here on earth, which is in essence to show the world the true meaning of Christ's love.

FIFTH WEEK OF EASTER – SATURDAY

Readings: Acts 16:1-10; John 15:18-21

The Churches grew strong in the faith and increased in numbers daily.
Acts 16:5

Luke relates in Acts how Paul for the first time encounters Timothy who would become his disciple and travelling companion, and later the recipient of two letters from Paul which form part of the New Testament Canon. They brought with them to each new centre of population the far-reaching decisions of the Apostolic Council in Jerusalem and were witness to the astonishing spread and growth of local Christian communities. Paul had intended to travel further to Asia, for until now his missionary endeavours were confined to what we understand today as Asia Minor, but in a vision which the Apostle interpreted as a sign from God he heard someone calling him to come to Macedonia, and therefore to the European mainland. Paul's arrival there would be a step of monumental importance for the Christian faith and eventually for the development of the future civilization of Europe. This initiative on the part of Paul to cross over and bring the gospel to the cities of Greece marked another decisive stage on Christianity's path to becoming a faith for all peoples. The Lord's command at his Ascension to preach the gospel to the uttermost parts of the earth was now being fulfilled (Acts 1:8).

As he prepares his disciples for their future ministry, Christ tells them of the hostility, even hatred, which awaits them. Throughout all four gospels we hear of the disciples being warned to expect the same treatment which Christ himself received. His choice of them as his followers and friends sets them over against the values and standards of this world. They may even find themselves regarded as enemies. A disciple of Christ will have to make choices which run contrary to current opinion. Discipleship brings with it a cost, even persecution, but this only reflects the fate which Christ himself suffered. In some respects his whole public ministry placed him on trial before the secular powers and religious authorities of his time. Christ succeeded with those in whom he found faith, but the hostility he experienced arose so often from unbelief. Similarly, where the word of his gospel falls on the fertile ground of faith the disciples will know success, but they too are destined to encounter the dark mystery of unbelief in their work of preaching the gospel. Christ ascribes this unbelieving attitude on the part of those who reject both him and his disciples to ignorance of God his Father who sent him into the world. Running through this discourse of Christ is a thread of sadness that his own people have failed to recognise him as their Saviour and Messiah.

Readings: Acts 8:5-8, 14-17; 1 Peter 3:15-18;
John 14:15-21

*Then they laid hands on them and
they received the Holy Spirit.*
Acts 8:17

The persecution which followed the death of Stephen
in Jerusalem forced many believers to flee to the neighbouring regions. Philip the deacon went to a Samaritan
town where he preached the gospel and healed the sick
and those tormented by evil spirits. At the beginning of
Acts the risen Christ commissioned his disciples to be
his witnesses in Judea, Samaria, and to the ends of the
earth (Acts 1:8). With Philip's presence in Samaria the
spread of the gospel had taken a decisive step forward.
Luke highlights the central and indispensable role of the
apostles when he relates that Peter and John, two of the
Twelve, came down to Samaria and conferred the gift
of the Holy Spirit on the newly-baptised believers. As
the appointed figures of authority in the early Church it
was their prerogative to pass on what they had received
from the Lord, and to give their official approval to the
manner and direction in which the mission of the Church
was developing.

The communities to whom the apostle Peter addressed his First Letter lived in a hostile environment as Christians. He counsels them to be ready with an answer for those who seek the reasons for their Christian way of life. Peter is urging believers to develop what would later be termed a Christian apologetic, exhorting them to defend their faith with courtesy and respect for those with whom they engaged in dialogue. He declares that the witness of a good life is the best defence against those who slander them. The advice of Peter to these new Christians retains a remarkable relevance, even after two thousand years. Should Christians have to suffer for their faith, they should look to the example of Christ whose innocent death opened up the way to God for all of us.

Jesus tells his disciples that the proof of their love for him will be the extent to which they live according to his teaching. He promises that another Paraclete will come in his place once he has gone, which he calls the Spirit of truth. His own presence among them has been of limited duration, whereas the Spirit of truth will remain with them always. The disciples and those who follow them can be secure that they are walking in the way of Christ through the indwelling of the Holy Spirit. The term Paraclete has no exact equivalent in English and we might understand it best as someone who stands alongside the disciples to keep them in the truth of Jesus and preserve them from false doctrine. The affectionate sentiment of Christ that he would not leave his disciples orphans suggests that the Holy Spirit will continue to make Christ's presence a reality for the Church. He will finally return in judgement to bring them home to unending life, and then they will discover the reality of that unity he enjoys with the Father and the Holy Spirit.

SIXTH SUNDAY OF EASTER – YEAR B

Readings: Acts 10:25-26,34-35,44-48; 1 John 4:7-10;
John 15:9-17

*Peter declared, 'In truth I have come to realise that
God has no favourites.'*
Acts 10:34

The well-known story of the conversion of the centurion
Cornelius illustrates how the early Church, here in the
person of Peter, grew in its understanding of the Christian
gospel. Until this point they had confined their preaching
to those of Jewish background, now they were compelled
to enlarge their horizons. Cornelius is described as God-
fearing but not a Jew, yet Peter is directed by God in
a vision to go to his house. While Peter was speaking,
the Holy Spirit came down on Cornelius and those with
him, evoking memories of the day of Pentecost. The
astonished Peter now realised that it was the divine will
for the pagans to hear the good news of Christ, as well
as those who were born Israelites. The chief apostle gave
orders for Cornelius and household to be baptised there
and then. In Acts, Luke devotes considerable space to the
whole Cornelius episode which suggests he considered
it to be an event of great significance. The baptism of
Cornelius and his family moves the young Church a step
further along the path that would ultimately lead to the
mission to all nations.

One gets the impression that in his letter, John, a figure of authority, is speaking intimately to friends. His language is simple but profound and appears to come from someone who has long reflected on the person of Jesus Christ and the message he left us. Love, says John, pervades this whole message from beginning to end. The source of all love is God, and the proof of that love is that he sent his own beloved Son into the world as a sin offering. What greater evidence of God's love do we require? John goes so far as to say that God himself is love, a love which has embraced us before we ourselves were ever capable of loving God in return. The reference to Christ as a sin-offering underlines the sacrificial nature of the divine love in giving his Son. Our love for one another, asserts John, must be marked by that same sacrificial dimension.

The theme of mutual love dominates this section of Christ's farewell discourse to his apostles. It is also a teaching intended for the Church of all time. The Christian life is expressed here in terms of love and friendship. But the love of which Jesus speaks belongs to another order, for the love which his disciples should show to one another is in some way part of that divine love which the Father has for his Son Jesus. When we keep Christ's commandments we are reflecting the divine love that is within us. And lest we romanticise this love, Christ expounds what is the supreme example of divine love: to lay down his life for his friends. St Paul would later observe that love never comes to an end (1 Cor 13:8), and it is this kind of mutual love which ought to permeate the life of Christ's friends, in imitation of his own love for us.

SIXTH SUNDAY OF EASTER – YEAR C

Readings: Acts 15:1-2,22-29; Apocalypse 21:10-14,22-23;
John 14:23-29

*And the walls of the city had twelve
foundation stones, each one of which bore the name
of one of the twelve apostles of the Lamb.*
Apocalypse 21:14

[First Reading: see Friday of Fifth Week, p.100]

John the visionary describes the future under God using
the image of a new and eternal Jerusalem. He portrays
the splendour of the city and its radiant glory in terms of
the most precious jewels and diamonds. Employing highly
metaphorical language he states that inscribed over the
gates of the city were the names of the twelve tribes of
Israel, while written on the foundations' stones were those
of the twelve apostles of the Lamb. The combination of
both sets of names as integral to the city represents the
unity of God's plan of salvation for the human race as
recorded in Scripture, beginning with the Patriarchs and
reaching its climax with the twelve apostles chosen by
Jesus Christ. Central to his new and final dispensation
sketched here would be the presence of God and the
Lamb. The regular pattern of days and months, marked
by the sun and the moon, which regulate our lives here
on earth would no longer obtain. The eternal light of the
divine glory and that of the victorious Lamb would usher

in an entirely new and blessed life, something at present grasped by faith alone.

In his farewell address Jesus is directing his words to the Eleven gathered in the Upper Room, but his teaching is intended for the wider community of all who would come to believe in him, the Church. The touchstone of genuine love for Christ is the observance of all he has taught them. Just as he comes from God, so everything that he speaks and does is of God. John the Evangelist, whose gospel has been described as being 'spiritual' in character, highlights the indwelling presence of the Father and the Son in the heart of the true believer. The final words of the risen Christ to his disciples in Matthew's Gospel come to mind here, 'I am with you all days, until the end of the world' (28:20). The eleven apostles were not yet in a position to understand the full meaning of all Jesus was saying to them; they would eventually be led into a deeper appreciation through the Holy Spirit whom Jesus promises to send from the Father. An important corollary of this promise is that the Spirit constantly inspires the Church of every age with fresh insights into Christ's gospel. Moreover, the guidance of the Spirit of the Father and the Son ensures that she will always remain faithful to the deposit of truth entrusted to her by Christ.

SIXTH WEEK OF EASTER – MONDAY

Readings: Acts 16:11-15; John 15:26–16:4

And you will be my witnesses,
because you have been with me from the beginning.
John 15:27

Paul's first important stop on reaching the European mainland was the city of Philippi, a Roman centre of considerable significance. From the language used in our text, it would appear that Luke, the author of Acts, accompanied him on this journey. Paul took the message of the gospel to a group of women gathered at a customary place of prayer by the river. A woman who was well-known in the purple-dye trade was particularly receptive to his preaching and became a believer. In a passing but notable comment, Luke tells us that the Lord had opened Lydia's heart to what Paul was saying with the result that she and her household were baptised. The missionary outreach of Paul and the early Church was only made possible through the activity of divine grace at work deep in the hearts of those who heard the apostles preach. The fact that Lydia offered the hospitality of her house to Paul, presumably for further explanation of the whole Christian gospel, implies that the Apostle was now firmly established in Europe and that his ministry was already bearing fruit.

Jesus returns again to the theme of the Paraclete or Advocate, the Holy Spirit, whom he will send to the disciples from the Father. As the Spirit of truth, the Paraclete will lead and guide the disciples into a fuller understanding of all that Jesus taught them. The Trinitarian dimension which forms the backdrop to the mission of Jesus Christ is very evident here. The Father and the Holy Spirit make possible and cooperate as a unity in the saving work of Jesus and may never be dissociated from that work. The function of the Holy Spirit will be to witness to Jesus and we may well wonder whether Christ is alluding here to the hidden activity of the Spirit throughout the world in ways we don't understand. The apostles too were to be the first and irreplaceable witnesses to Jesus because they had accompanied him from the beginning of his ministry. They, with the bishops as their successors, would be the guarantors of what we call the deposit of faith. Having been an eye-witness to the earthly ministry of Jesus was an indispensable qualification for an apostle, as is evident when the Eleven met to choose a successor to Judas (Acts 1:21-22). The future scenario facing the apostles which Jesus goes on to describe will be one marked by rejection, even martyrdom. Those who perpetrate such terrible deeds will do so out of ignorance and misplaced zeal because they have failed to recognise the truth about Jesus as the Son of the Father. Jesus forewarns the apostles what they can expect.

Readings: Acts 16:22-34; John 16:5-11

*For the prince of this world has already
been condemned.*
John 16:11

During his stay in Philippi Paul fell victim to mob violence
and, sharing the fate of Christ himself and that of Peter
earlier (Acts 12:1-11), was beaten and thrown into
prison. Undaunted, together with his companion Silas
he prayed and sang praises to God. As he would remark
later to Timothy (2 Tim 2:9), the word of God cannot
be chained. An earthquake shook the prison and Paul
and his fellow prisoners found themselves at liberty. The
distraught gaoler was on the point of committing suicide
but was prevented from doing so by Paul who took the
opportunity to evangelise and baptise him, together
with his whole household. The harsh treatment and
imprisonment which Paul endured shows how the gospel
was planted at great personal cost to the Apostle. Yet
the trials and tribulations which he faced never appeared
to discourage him or deflect him from his evangelical
zeal, or ultimately from his love for the Son of God. The
incident at Philippi also illustrates how the victory of
Christ crucified over the power of sin and evil continues to
make itself felt in the life of the young missionary Church.

Faith in the Lord's definitive triumph sustains the Church in every generation.

Christ unfolds to the disciples the reason for his imminent departure from among them. They are despondent at the prospect, but in truth his leaving them will be to their benefit. In the divine economy of salvation the Holy Spirit can come only when Jesus is no longer visibly with them. The connection between Jesus leaving his disciples and the coming of the Paraclete is to be explained in terms of his suffering and redemptive death on the cross. He must first be glorified through death before the Spirit can be given. At the moment of his death the Evangelist John notes that Jesus gave up his spirit (19:30), an implicit allusion to the truth that the gift of the Holy Spirit comes to us through the One crucified on the cross. The outpouring of the promised Spirit will have grave consequences for the world, for he will inspire the Church to proclaim the sinfulness of deliberate disbelief in Christ, now the risen Son of God. The righteousness of Jesus' claim to be the Son of God will be proved by his Ascension and return to the Father in glory. Finally, the whole sequence of his passion, death and resurrection will be a judgement of condemnation on the prince of evil, who until now has held the whole world in his grasp. The disciples will come to comprehend the truth of Christ's words only through their own faith and the inspiration of the Holy Spirit.

SIXTH WEEK OF EASTER – WEDNESDAY

Readings: Acts 17:15,22-18,1; John 16:12-15

In fact, He is not far from any of us.
Acts 17:27

Paul's second great speech in Acts is addressed to the leading citizens of Athens. Luke presents a dramatic picture of the Apostle taking the gospel of Christ into the heart of a city famous for its distinguished tradition of culture and philosophical speculation. Paul attempts to speak to the Athenians in a language which they would understand, and we have here an example of how the first Christian missionaries engaged in dialogue with the predominantly Greek culture of their time. Paul admires the religious zeal of the Athenians, in particular their openness to the transcendent, exemplified in their erection of an altar to the unknown God. This in truth is the God whom the Apostle proclaims to them, a God who is the creator of the universe and who bestows blessing on all the nations of the earth, and a God who is close to each member of the human race, as even one of their poets wrote. He is unseen, yet has now spoken through a man whom Paul has come to speak about, who has been raised from the dead and will one day return as judge of the world. Paul's mention of the resurrection of the dead and eternal life proved offensive to the philosophically minded Athenians and they scoffed at the idea. Although the Apostle appeared to have had limited success in Athens, the encounter of the Christian faith with the inheritors of the Greek philosophical tradition would mark an important step forward for the Church in her mission to the Gentiles.

Jesus has much more to say to his disciples, but they are unable to take any more and further clarification of his words would be the work of the Spirit. The role of the Spirit will be to lead the disciples into the deeper truth of the identity of Jesus as Son of the Father and to the true significance of his passion, death and resurrection. The disciples need have no fear that the Spirit will mislead them. As the Spirit of the Father and Son he must necessarily speak only of the things of God. With the full enlightenment of the Holy Spirit at Pentecost the believing Church will worship the glorified and risen Christ. His promptings will be the sure guide for the disciples along the path which Jesus has laid out for them. These gospel verses contain a rich and complex teaching on the part the Holy Spirit will play in the future internal life of the Church and in her relationship to the world. We are also given an insight into the intimacy and mutual sharing within that ineffable union which binds together the Father, Son and Holy Spirit, and which we know as the Most Holy Trinity. The Christian community for all time is greatly privileged to listen to these sublime words of Jesus spoken in the Upper Room.

Readings: Acts 18:1-8; John 16:16-20

I can now go to the Gentiles with a clear conscience.
Acts 16:6

[When the Ascension of the Lord is celebrated today,
use the meditations on pages 124-9]

On leaving Athens Paul went to Corinth, a city where
he would subsequently spend over a year in the work of
evangelisation. He later wrote at least two letters to the
Church in Corinth. The Apostle had a gift for friendship,
and Priscilla and Aquila ranked among the many friends
he made on his travels. Their names occur again in a list
of greetings in his Letter to the Romans (16:1-16). We
are told that Paul was a tentmaker by trade, a profession
he continued to practice even after his conversion since it
gave him a sense of independence wherever he preached
the gospel. He was well aware of the Lord's word that
the labourer was worthy of his hire, but he preferred not
to make use of the privilege (1 Cor 9:12-16). Luke records
yet again the opposition the Apostle encountered in
proclaiming Christ as the Messiah which was a recurring
theme wherever he went, in particular from those of
a Jewish background. Such challenges served only to
strengthen his resolve to bring the good news of Jesus
to the pagans. The conversion of the president of the

synagogue, followed by many other Corinthians, testifies to the power and persuasion of Paul the preacher.

The disciples expressed puzzlement at the apparent enigmatic nature of Jesus' words to the effect that in a short time they would no longer see him, but again in a little while they would see him. John the Evangelist often highlights the extraordinary knowledge which Jesus has of people and so he already knows the questions which the disciples would like to put to him. By these words Christ is clearly alluding to his coming departure, to his passion and death, and to his return in the resurrection. He is going to his Father, but in the language of the Fourth Gospel, that must be by way of the cross and resurrection. The disciples have not yet grasped the meaning of what Jesus is saying to them, yet instead of answering their question directly he warns them of an approaching period of sorrow and distress. For a time it will seem to them as if the powers of this world have triumphed and all their hopes dashed. Yet Jesus promises that their period of mourning will not last, in fact it will be transformed into joy. The joy of which he speaks is that of his resurrection from the dead and his final victory over sin, evil and death. The disciples will come to know the truth of Jesus' words only when the sadness of Calvary is followed by his appearance among them on Easter evening as the risen Lord (Jn 20:19-23).

Readings: Acts 18:9-18; John 16:20-23

Do not be afraid,
but speak out and do not be silent.
Acts 18:9

Throughout Scripture the Lord often revealed himself
and his counsel to his chosen ones by means of dreams,
and while in Corinth Paul's apostolic commission was
renewed in a dream. He was to be fearless in speaking
about Christ, for there were many in the city already
touched by God's grace and who would be receptive
to Paul's proclamation of the Christian gospel. That he
stayed there for eighteen months is an indication of both
his determination and patient work among his Corinthian
converts. Paul's missionary endeavours often encountered
intrigue and the threat of violence, and his experiences
in Corinth were no exception. His Jewish adversaries
had the Apostle brought before the Roman Proconsul,
accusing him of teaching alternative ways to worship
God and so being in violation of the Law of Moses. On
this occasion Paul was acquitted since the Proconsul
clearly judged that what was in dispute was a matter of
interpretation concerning Jewish beliefs and not a legal
issue of public interest. In relating this episode Luke,
the author of Acts, is at pains to make clear that Paul's
activity as an evangelist in no way contravened public

order. The opposition to him arose out of jealousy on the part of those who felt he was distorting the traditions of the Jewish faith.

Jesus compares the crisis which will shortly befall the disciples to the experiences of a woman in childbirth. Scripture employs the image of birth pangs to denote a time of dramatic, even cosmic upheaval (Isa 21:3; 1 Thess 5:3). The trauma experienced by the disciples at the arrest and execution of Jesus will be comparable to the pain and distress of a woman in the throes of becoming a mother. Yet once she has given birth she quickly forgets her sufferings in the joy that a new human being has come into the world. The disciples will soon find themselves in a period of confusion and acute distress because their Master will be suddenly wrenched from them. Already a sense of sadness and apprehension has overtaken them, but Christ assures them that they will see him again and the sorrow they knew will be turned into unbounded joy. The glory of Christ's resurrection will cast a completely new light on all that they have suffered through their despair over his death. He will come among them once more, this time for ever. Then they will have a deeper understanding and appreciation of the divine plan which unfolded in Jesus Christ. There will be no need for any further questions.

Readings: Acts 18:23-28; John 16:23-28

Ask and you will receive,
so that your joy may be complete.
John 16:24

The wide sweep of Paul's missionary travels is mentioned almost in passing by Luke. Even by today's standards the distances covered by the Apostle were remarkable. Here he touches the Galatian country, and he would later write a letter to the Church in Galatia. Our reading today concerns a figure of some importance in the early spread of the gospel, Apollos who came from the city of Alexandria in Egypt which had a large Greek-speaking Jewish population, renowned for their knowledge and study of the Scriptures. Apart from being well-versed in the Scriptures, Apollos was remarkable for his knowledge of the Christian faith and especially about the Lord Jesus, yet he had only received the baptism administered by John. The call to repentance and baptismal practice of John had obviously spread far beyond Palestine and was a measure of the impact the Baptist had among those, such as Apollos, who would eventually become believers in Christ. Paul's friends, Priscilla and Aquila, completed what was missing in Apollos' knowledge of the faith. He subsequently became a staunch apologist and used his familiarity with the Scriptures of Israel to demonstrate that Jesus was in truth the Christ.

Anticipating the future and the time following his passion and death, Jesus refers with emphasis to his role as mediator with the Father. In days to come he will no longer be present to his disciples visibly, in bodily form, but his care and concern for them will remain just as effective, though exercised in an altogether different manner. It is in accordance with these words of Jesus that the Church from earliest times has concluded her prayers with the formula, 'Through Christ our Lord.' Once the appointed hour of his death and resurrection has come to pass his teaching, formerly expressed in parables and enigmatic sayings, will be understood in a new light. Through the guidance and inspiration of the Holy Spirit which Jesus has promised to send the disciples they will then grasp in its fullness what Paul would later describe as 'the mystery of Christ' (Rom 16:25). At the heart of that mystery is the love of the Father which embraces those who accept and believe in his Son. Jesus is now returning to the Father, but he will do so freely and without human constraint. His passage to the Father through his cross and death will be a sovereign act of his own time and choosing.

THE ASCENSION OF THE LORD – YEAR A

Readings: Acts 1:1-11; Ephesians 1:17-23; Matthew 28:16-20

Behold, I am with you all days,
even to the end of the age.
Matthew 28:20

[When the Ascension of the Lord is celebrated on
the previous Thursday, use the meditations in the Appendix]

Luke begins the Acts of the Apostles with an account of the Ascension of the Lord Jesus. A new age was about to break, that of the Church, but for that to happen Christ tells the disciples that they must first remain in Jerusalem and await the promised Holy Spirit. Christ contrasts the baptism in water conferred by John with another and greater baptism, which was the work of the Spirit. The still earthbound outlook of the apostles is reflected in their question to Jesus as to when he was going to restore the kingdom of Israel. Jesus says that is the prerogative of his Father alone. Their Spirit-inspired mission will be to take his gospel to all nations. As he ascends and disappears from their view, the apostles are assured by angels that the same Lord will one day return in glory.

The reading from the Letter to the Ephesians forms part of a prayer of Paul for his readers. It is the Apostle's wish that they grow ever more in their knowledge and appreciation of what faith in Christ means, and in particular of the hope it offers. Speaking of the Ascension, Paul envisages Christ in a triumphal procession subduing all the alien and hostile forces which rule the universe, and taking his place in glory at the Father's right hand. He is now the king of creation, and is present with all his power in a unique way in the members of his Church, which Paul describes as his Body and he the Head.

The final scene in Matthew's Gospel takes place on a mountain, appropriately so. Throughout his gospel the Evangelist has depicted Jesus as another and greater Moses. On Mount Sinai God appeared to Moses and gave him the commandments which would guide Israel. The Sermon on the Mount (Mt 5–7) depicts Jesus propounding his commandments and teaching. The parting words of Jesus prior to his Ascension form the great commission. The apostles are to evangelise all nations, to baptise them and to pass on the teaching they received from Jesus. Faced with a task of such magnitude they, and the Church after them, have the assurance of Christ's enduring presence as long as time lasts.

Readings: Acts 1:1-11; Ephesians 4:1-13; Mark 16:15-20

He who has descended is the one who has also
ascended above all the heavens.
Ephesians 4:10

[First Reading: see Year A, p.124]

[When the Ascension of the Lord is celebrated on
the previous Thursday, use the meditations in the Appendix]

This passage from Paul's Letter to the Ephesians has
clearly been chosen for today's feast because of its
references to Christ's descent to what are described as
the lower parts of the earth, followed by his ascension
above all the heavens. These references would later form
part of our Creed. Applying a quotation from Psalm 68 to
Christ's death and rising, the Apostle speaks of the risen
Christ pouring out his gifts upon the community of the
Church, structuring it to be effective in its work of ministry
and contributing to its up-building. Pursuing a vein of
thought difficult for us to grasp fully, Paul teaches that the
risen and ascended Christ now fills the whole of creation
and that we, the members of the Church, are constantly
advancing in our knowledge and union with him.

The Evangelist Mark is characteristically brief in his
account of the final words and Ascension of the Lord
Jesus. The disciples' mandate to proclaim the gospel to

the whole world is close to the great commission found at the close of Matthew's Gospel. The Eleven are to go out to teach and baptise, and will share the same power to heal the sick and expel evil spirits as he had during his public ministry. What is implied here is that despite his bodily departure Christ will still remain very close to the apostles in their work of evangelisation. The description Mark gives of the Lord's Ascension is a dense statement of faith. Christ has been taken up to heaven and now sits at the favoured right hand of his Father, but at the same time continues his work as saviour in the world through the preaching and ministry of his disciples, which means in effect his Church.

THE ASCENSION OF THE LORD – YEAR C

Readings: Acts 1:1-11;
Hebrews 9:24-28, 10:19-23; Luke 24:46-53

*As he blessed them, he withdrew from them
and was taken up into heaven.*
Luke 24:51

[First Reading: see Year A, p.124]

[When the Ascension of the Lord is celebrated on
the previous Thursday, use the meditations in the Appendix]

Central to the Letter to the Hebrews is the figure of Jesus as the supreme high priest, our mediator with God. His Ascension is presented as an entry into the heavenly sanctuary to intercede with God on our behalf. Unlike the succession of earthly priests who have to offer sacrifice regularly for themselves and for the people, his single sacrifice of himself is efficacious for all time. We too can now be confident because we have gained access to God through that self-offering of Christ and the shedding of his blood. Although ascended, he remains our high priest and through faith we are united with him in God's heavenly sanctuary.

The Gospel of Luke ends on a note of joy. The risen Lord stands among his disciples and reaffirms to them that his passion and death were part of the divine plan to bring salvation to all nations. They are to be witnesses to the truth of these events. But they can succeed only in their work of evangelisation through the power and assistance of the Holy Spirit which Jesus promises will come to them in Jerusalem. The city of Jerusalem will appropriately mark the starting point for the proclamation of the gospel. The final gesture of Jesus to his disciples before his departure was one of blessing, a sign of his favour and his abiding affection for them. Luke notes how the Ascension did not leave the disciples dispirited; in fact they returned to the city full of joy. A new age had begun!

SEVENTH WEEK OF EASTER – MONDAY

Readings: Acts 19:1-8; John 16:29-33

Be confident! I have overcome the world.
John 16:33

Luke relates that during his sojourn in Ephesus Paul encountered a group of believers in Jesus whose faith, like that of Apollos, was incomplete, for they were unaware of the existence of the Holy Spirit. On hearing that they had been baptised by John, Paul took the opportunity to give a succinct account of the mission of John the Baptist, familiar to us from the gospels. John's baptism, Paul declared, represented a call to repentance and was a summons to prepare spiritually for the one who would follow John, Jesus Christ. The rite administered by John at the river Jordan was penitential by nature and a baptism in water only. The Christ whom John heralded would offer something far superior: baptism in the Holy Spirit. The Apostle is here stating the mind of the early Church leaders as to the value and place of John's preaching and baptism. They were at pains to stress the important but ultimately subsidiary part John had to play as he prepared the way for the coming of the Saviour. When Paul baptised this group of twelve men they had an experience similar to that of the apostles and disciples at Pentecost, and they found themselves speaking in tongues through the outpouring of the Holy Spirit.

As the long discourse of Jesus after the Last Supper draws to a close, the disciples confess that they now understand much more clearly what he has been saying to them. They also, and perhaps over-confidently, profess their faith in his divinity, as the one who has come from God. Christ tells them bluntly that the gravity of his hour which is imminent will find him alone, while they will abandon him to his fate. Yet the faith and conviction of Jesus shine through in his declared belief that his Father will always stand by him. The disciples should not be surprised at the dreadful events which are soon to befall him. He knows of them beforehand and remains composed. In spite of the chaos around them the disciples also are to be at peace within themselves, as he himself is. Whatever may happen to them externally because of the hatred and opposition from the hostile powers of this world they must not be unduly perturbed. The foundation for such confidence is that by embracing the cross on his path to glory he has overcome all that could harm and destroy them. His victory is their victory. His life's work, culminating in his passion, has been to defeat those ancient enemies, sin and death, which Christ here calls the world.

Readings: Acts 20:17-27; John 17:1-11

*For I have not wavered in placing before you
the whole of God's purpose.*
Acts 20:27

In his farewell address to the elders of the Church at
Ephesus Luke portrays the apostle Paul as an ideal pastor
of his flock and the model of a true Christian leader.
In a style reminiscent of Samuel's leave – taking of the
leadership of Israel (1 Sam 12:1-5), Paul lays bare his
deepest feelings as he sets before the Church leaders the
struggles and trials he has undergone in order to plant the
gospel of Christ among them. He has not spared himself
in their service. Through the grace of the Holy Spirit
at work in him he is now aware that he faces a future
marked by uncertainty, imprisonment and persecution.
His single overriding desire is remain faithful to the
charge laid on him by the risen Lord, that of spreading
the news of God's grace now given to the world in Christ.
Luke furnishes us in this passage with a quite remarkable
portrait of Paul as a faithful shepherd of those Churches
entrusted to his care and whom he has brought to birth
in Christ. In heartfelt sentiments expressed to those he
has commissioned to carry on his work as shepherds, the
Apostle examines his conscience publicly and confesses

that he has done his utmost to discharge his ministry faithfully before God.

Chapter seventeen of John's Gospel has been called the 'High Priestly Prayer of Jesus', since Christ is presented as interceding with his Father on behalf of his disciples. The words of Jesus are both moving and sublime and may be seen as his parting legacy to his friends. His hour, the beginning of his path to glory, has finally come and through it will his Father be glorified too. But as he enters into this sacred hour his prayer is for his disciples, that they too may come to share his glory in eternal life. When Jesus confesses to his Father that he has accomplished the work he came to do, the Evangelist depicts him speaking, as it were, from beyond his passion and death and as the Lord already in glory at the right hand of his Father. He prays that he may regain the glory of his divinity which was rightly his from eternity, and was hidden when, as the Word, he became flesh and lived among us (Jn 1:14). He declares before God that his chosen circle of friends, and by inference the subsequent Church, have come to know and believe that he is truly the Son of the Father. Once he has departed the disciples will have to face the hostile world, and so he prays for them. At the heart of this great prayer of Jesus is the glory of the Father and the future welfare of the disciples. In the thought and language of John, God the Father will be glorified through the cross of his Son. The Father and the Son will also be glorified through the work of the disciples and the Church on earth.

Readings: Acts 20:28-38; John 17:11-19

*Be on your guard for yourselves and for
the whole flock, over which the Holy Spirit has
placed you as overseers.*
Acts 20:28

In language which echoes that of Christ himself when
speaking of the Good Shepherd (Jn 10), Paul warns
the leaders of the Churches in Ephesus to be vigilant
because the flock they have been appointed to lead has
been purchased at the price of Christ's own blood. The
dangers will be many, especially from those who would
try to infiltrate and mislead people with their erroneous
teachings. Already we can note the concern that the
integrity of the faith be preserved and safeguarded by
those charged with positions of responsibility in the
various ecclesial communities. The exemplary personal
witness given by the Apostle himself over three years
ought to inspire and encourage the elders, and Paul
reminds them of how he scrupulously earned his own
keep in order to assist the poor. In support of this practice
he quotes a saying of the Lord not found elsewhere, that it
is better to give than to receive. The affectionate farewell
given to Paul by the leaders of the Church at Ephesus
testifies to the esteem and respect in which they held the
great Apostle. It also highlights his warm human qualities

and gift for friendship which he brought to his missionary apostolate.

Christ prays to his Father to keep his disciples in his name, in other words to protect and keep them safe by his divine power. The address to his Father as 'holy' reminds us of the second line of the 'Our Father', and echoes of that same prayer are to be heard throughout this magnificent priestly prayer of Jesus. In plain but astonishing language, Christ prays that the bonds existing among his disciples be a reflection of that most intimate and ineffable unity which he enjoys with the Father. The Church's later understanding of baptism would teach that as a community we are given a share in this Trinitarian divine life of which Christ speaks. Foreseeing a troubled and difficult way ahead in the world for his followers, Christ beseeches the Father to protect them from the evil one who will remain active and threatening. Their spiritual values and faith in him as God's Son and Saviour will set them apart from the world, just as he himself found himself at odds with the world and society of his day. They are to continue the mission which the Father gave him, sanctified in the assurance of divine truth. The foundation of their consecration in truth will be rooted in Christ's own act of obedience and consecration to his Father's will in the self-abasement of his suffering and death. By their sacramental sharing in Christ's cross, believers too will be consecrated in God's truth.

Readings: Acts 22:30, 23:6-11; John 17:20-26

Courage! Just as you have borne witness to me in Jerusalem, so now you must do the same in Rome.
Acts 23:11

In Jerusalem, Paul again finds himself maltreated by an angry crowd who were outraged both by the account of his conversion and his boldness in preaching in the Temple precincts. In a parallel with the Passion of Christ, the Apostle is brought before the whole body of the Jewish authorities where he skilfully defends himself by exploiting the opposing views of the Pharisees who professed belief in the resurrection of the dead, and the Sadducees who maintained that there is no afterlife of any kind. Paul claimed that he was on trial for his faith in the resurrection of the dead. Feelings were running high between the opposing factions and a riot threatened, with Paul in danger of his life. The Roman tribune intervened just in time and placed Paul in prison. Divine reassurance came to Paul from the Lord in a dream, and he was told that having witnessed to Christ in Jerusalem he must now do the same in Rome. The two cities are symbolic and significant. Paul had proclaimed Jesus as Saviour and Messiah in the city of David, the religious centre of the Jewish people. His final journey would take him to the heart of world political power, imperial Rome, and there too he would be unrelenting in his efforts to preach the Good News of the gospel of Jesus Christ.

Christ concludes his great prayer to his Father by embracing those who afterwards will believe the preaching of the apostles and form the historical Church. His earnest desire is for them to remain united among themselves, in imitation of the oneness existing between himself and his Father. Such a unity of faith and love will be a powerful witness to the truth of his mission as the Son of God. By revealing the Father to his disciples through word and sign in the course of his ministry, Christ has at the same time shared the divine glory with them. The humanity of Jesus is transparent in his request that his chosen friends join him in that divine glory which is properly his from eternity. It is there that the true identity of their Master will be fully disclosed to them. The world has not accepted the claim of Jesus that he has come from the Father and so has not known him. The disciples have accepted Jesus' word and his revelation of the Father to them, and he promises to continue that mission of deepening their knowledge about his Father, which is the knowledge of God's love for them. This ongoing work of teaching in the life of the Church will be accomplished by the Spirit of the Father and the Son who, in the words of Paul, 'is the love of God poured into our hearts' (Rom 5:5).

Readings: Acts 25:13-21; John 21:15-19

Simon, son of John,
do you love me more than these?
John 21:15

Luke continues his account of Paul's final days in Palestine with the Apostle being brought before King Agrippa to answer charges brought against him by the religious and civil authorities in Jerusalem. The Roman rulers were baffled by what appeared to them as disputes over the finer points of Jewish religious faith and wanted to send Paul back to Jerusalem to have his case resolved. The author of Acts is here implying Paul's innocence where Roman law was concerned, and the real reason for his trial was because of his belief in Jesus Christ as the Son of God. Paul had argued and preached from place to place, as the fuller history of Acts relates, that Jesus was the fulfilment of the promises God had made to Israel through the patriarchs and prophets. He was the Messiah his people had long awaited and hoped for. Being born in Tarsus, Paul enjoyed Roman citizenship and he invokes this privilege by asking to have his case heard at the imperial court of the Emperor himself. His wish was granted and he began his last missionary journey, as a prisoner, to Rome. The words of the risen Lord to Ananias at the time of Paul's conversion have come to pass, 'This man is my chosen instrument to bear my name before the Gentiles, kings and the sons of Israel' (Acts 9:15).

The gospel story, set by the Sea of Galilee, takes the form of a question and answer dialogue between the risen Christ and the apostle Peter. The threefold question of the Lord to Peter as to whether he loves him corresponds to the triple denial of Peter at the time of his passion. The favoured Scriptural pastoral images of the shepherd and sheep again recur, but this time with a difference. When Peter responded affirmatively to Jesus' question he is enjoined each time to feed his flock. Christ is now passing on the care of his flock to Peter. Once Peter confessed to loving the Lord to a degree more than the other disciples he was affirmed in the role of shepherd. After his denials, he had now been re-commissioned in his place of seniority among the other apostles. This seniority is often described as the primacy of Peter. In a comment on this passage, St Augustine makes the telling point that although Peter is the shepherd the sheep nonetheless still belong to Christ. The scene ends with the Lord alluding to what the future holds for Peter. As a young man he followed a path of his own choosing; it will be otherwise when he is old. The Evangelist notes that Jesus was foretelling the martyrdom of Peter.

SEVENTH WEEK OF EASTER – SATURDAY

Readings: Acts 28:16-20,30-31; John 21:20-25

*It is because of the hope of Israel
that I wear this chain.*
Acts 28:20

The story that the Acts of the Apostles encompasses
closes with the apostle Paul under house arrest in
Rome. After a tumultuous and eventful sea passage
which climaxed in a shipwreck on the island of Malta,
Paul finally arrives as a prisoner in the capital city of the
Roman Empire. His apostolic zeal remained undiminished
and he continued to speak of Christ to all who came to
visit him. In accordance with his custom of first addressing
his own people, he summoned the leading Jewish citizens
in the city, giving the reasons for his captivity and for his
presence in Rome. Protesting his innocence, Paul states
that the true cause for his predicament is the one who
is the object of Israel's hope, the Messiah, Jesus Christ.
Luke gives a favourable account of the time Paul was
in captivity, remarking that he was at liberty to receive
visitors and to preach to them about the Lord Jesus, and
the kingdom of God which he came to proclaim and
establish. Luke opens his account of the history of the
first Christian community with the commission Christ
gave to his disciples prior to his Ascension, 'You will be
my witnesses in Jerusalem, in the whole of Judea and

Samaria, and to the ends of the earth' (Acts 1:8). For Luke, that commission has become a reality with the presence and preaching of Paul in Rome, the centre of world power and political authority.

The final verses of the Gospel of John concern Peter and the beloved disciple. Having been appointed shepherd of Christ's flock, Peter inquired of Jesus as to the future place of this disciple, identified as the one who leaned on the Lord's breast during the Last Supper and asked who it was who would betray him. As was often his custom, the Lord did not give a direct answer to Peter but made a somewhat opaque statement instead. That disciple would remain until Christ returned, though we are not given any further details. In any case, it was no concern of Peter's. He had his own personal vocation from the Lord. The Evangelist adds for the benefit of the reader that this did not mean the beloved disciple would not die. He also vouches for the truth and dependability of his gospel, and the community can endorse his witness. This most majestic of gospels began with the poem-prologue which culminates with the resounding declaration that the Word became flesh and lived among us (Jn 1:14). It now ends by claiming that all the books that could ever be written would not suffice to tell the full story of him who was the Word made flesh.

PENTECOST SUNDAY – YEAR A

Readings: Acts 2:1-11; 1 Corinthians 12:3-7,12-13;
John 20:19-23

*We hear them preaching in our own languages
the marvellous works of God.*
Acts 2:11

The extraordinary event that was Pentecost gave birth to the Church. The mighty wind and tongues of fire were symbols of the divine power that would infuse the apostles and the Church in their mission of proclaiming Jesus Christ as Lord to the world. In all four gospels Christ had promised that the Father would send the Holy Spirit in his name, and now that promise has come to pass. The Spirit so transformed the disciples that the courage and eloquence they previously lacked now became their hallmark. Luke, the author of Acts, relates that Jewish pilgrims present from many different nations heard the apostles speak about Christ in their own particular language. He probably has in mind the disunity of the human race from its early history as recorded in Genesis (11:1-9), when God confused and scattered humanity because of its pride. Now at Pentecost unity is again restored through the Holy Spirit when representatives of many nations could understand the one language of the gospel of Jesus Christ. With good reason the

Second Vatican Council could describe the Church as the Sacrament of Unity.

The apostle Paul had a keen awareness of the essential place of the Holy Spirit both in the life of the baptised Christian and in the Church at large. The anointing with the Holy Spirit conferred on believers at baptism enables them to make a full profession of faith in Jesus Christ as Lord and the Son of God. With the unity of the Church in mind, Paul teaches that the diversity of spiritual gifts which individual members of the Church enjoy have their single source in the Holy Spirit, and must therefore serve the common good. The Apostle introduces the concept of the Church as a single body with many parts. He is referring here to the Church as the Body of Christ into which believers are incorporated through baptism. This is a profound analogy which seeks to underline the mystery of the Church as the unity of the baptised in Christ, who have a mutual responsibility for each other. The safeguarding of that unity both in fidelity to the tradition of the apostles and the witness of the Christian life is the work of the Holy Spirit.

The Easter evening scene of the risen Lord encountering his disciples in the Upper Room presents us with John's understanding of the Holy Spirit and his function in the life of the Church. The Evangelist had noted earlier (Jn 7:39) that the Holy Spirit could be given only after

Jesus had been glorified. Now the victorious and glorious Jesus was able to share his life-giving Spirit with his disciples as he had promised. At the creation the Lord God breathed into the dust and created man (Gen 2:7); the Church is now the new creation animated by the Holy Spirit. The power of the Spirit, conferred by the risen Christ, will enable the Church to be the means of reconciliation between humanity and God, described here as the forgiveness of sins.

PENTECOST SUNDAY – YEAR B

Readings: Acts 2:1-11; Galatians 5:16-25;
John 15:26-27, 16:12-15

If we live by the Spirit,
let us conduct our lives according to the Spirit.
Galatians 5:25

[First Reading: see Year A, p.143]

In this well-known passage from his letter to the Galatians, where he contrasts a manner of life according to the desires of the flesh and one that is in accord with the promptings of the Holy Spirit, the apostle Paul teaches that the Spirit is the guiding principle of the moral life of a Christian. The psalm which opens the Book of Psalms describes the two and sharply different roads a person may take in life, one according to God's commandments, and the other according to the evil inclinations of the human heart. Paul employs a similar structure in his teaching to the Galatians. The marvellous roll call of gifts which the Spirit confers, love, joy, peace etc, throw into sharp relief the ongoing reality of the Holy Spirit in the life of the Church. The experience of the first Pentecost and the outpouring of the Holy Spirit continue to be replicated whenever a person is baptised in Christ, once crucified and now gloriously alive.

The Paraclete whom Jesus promises he will send from the Father will reveal the full truth about Jesus. The Spirit will bear witness to him by leading them into a fuller understanding of all that Jesus taught them. He will anoint them with God's truth (1 Jn 2:27) and preserve them from error and false doctrine. The apostles too, in conjunction with the Holy Sprit, must witness to Jesus for they have been his companions from the very outset. They will have the charism as authoritative interpreters of Jesus. In the atmospheric setting of the Upper Room the disciples were in no position to comprehend all that they were hearing from Jesus. That deeper insight into the truth of Jesus would only follow afterwards, in the light of his resurrection and the bestowal of the Holy Spirit. The words of Jesus here, referring to the Father, are of a piece with the theology of the fourth Gospel. He never acts independently of his Father and all that the Father has is his as well. Therefore the work of the Holy Spirit will, in effect, be a continuation of his work on earth, only now through the Church.

Readings: Acts 2:1-11; Romans 8:8-17;
John 14:15-16, 23-26

The Spirit of the Lord has filled the whole world.
Wisdom 1:7

[First Reading: see Year A, p.143]

Paul reflects on the role of the Holy Spirit in the Christian life in chapter 8 of his great letter to the Romans. It was God's Spirit, the Apostle says, who raised Jesus from the dead and as Christians we share in that same life-giving Spirit, and finally our mortal bodies will one day enjoy the fullness of the life which Christ now possesses. However, as long as we remain here there will always be a struggle between the Spirit and the desires of flesh, to which we must not surrender. Through the Spirit which we have received, we now stand in a wholly new relationship with God, no longer that of a slave or servant, but of a child of God. We have the privilege to address God with the same intimacy as Jesus did, Abba, Father. We form part of the family of God, and are therefore co-heirs with Christ of the glory that is one day to be revealed.

Christ has accompanied his disciples this far but now must leave them. He has until this time been their Advocate, but when he is gone he will send them another Advocate who will continue his work of instruction and guidance.

At present they are unable to grasp the full meaning of all that he has said and done while still with them. It will be the work of the Holy Spirit to lead them further into the truth of the true and full identity of Jesus, and what his death and resurrection signify for the world. Jesus' references to the Holy Spirit in John's Gospel make the Trinitarian dimension abundantly clear. The Spirit which the Father will send comes in his name.

Appendix

SEVENTH SUNDAY OF EASTER – YEAR A

Readings: Acts 1:12-14; 1 Peter 4:13-16; John 17:1-11

All were united in continuous prayer,
with several women and with Mary, the mother of
Jesus, and with his brothers.
Acts 1:14

This evocative vignette from the beginning of Acts depicts the apostles and followers of Jesus gathered in prayer in the Upper Room, the scene of the Last Supper and where Jesus spoke his parting words to his disciples. At his Ascension he had told them to remain in Jerusalem until they had received power from on high. Luke here makes specific mention of the presence of Mary and we would be justified in seeing in his description an image of the expectant Church assembled in prayer around Mary the Mother of the Lord, obedient to the Lord's command and awaiting the promised Holy Spirit. Catholic theology and Marian piety in the course of the centuries have found a deeper significance in the disciples united with Mary in prayer. Mary represents symbolically the woman who watches over and cares for the followers of her Son, hence the title now commonly ascribed to her, 'Mary, Mother of the Church.' A similar interpretation may be given to John's portrayal of Mary at the foot of the cross

(Jn 19:25-27), when Jesus entrusts his disciples to his mother in the person of the Beloved Disciple.

The apostle Peter offers a word of consolation and reassurance to those believers who are suffering hardship and contempt from those around them because of their Christian manner of life. At the same time he stresses a fundamental truth: to share in the sufferings of Christ will also bring a share in his glory. When Christian communities find their environment hostile and aggressive they can be assured of the comforting presence of God's Holy Spirit. Their moral behaviour however should not give any grounds for suspicion, but when they are wrongfully accused then they should glory in the fact that they are following in the footsteps of Christ who himself suffered unjustly.

[Gospel: see Tuesday of Seventh Week, p.132]

Readings: Acts 1:15-17, 20-26; 1 John 4:11-16;
John 17:11-19

The lot fell on Matthias,
and he was appointed one of the twelve apostles.
Acts 1:26

The care which the eleven apostles took to replace Judas is an indication of the obligation they felt to remain faithful to the pattern the Lord Jesus had established. He had chosen the Twelve, after the manner of the twelve sons of Jacob who became the ancestors of the people of Israel. The apostles would be the representatives of the new Israel, the Church. Peter supports his action with a quotation from Psalm 109, v.8, to show that it was in conformity with the will of God as recorded in Scripture. The one chosen must meet certain requirements: that he was actually a companion of the Lord Jesus throughout his public ministry, and a witness to his passion, death, resurrection and ascension. In other words, he would be a bearer of the apostolic tradition and a guarantor of the truth of what Jesus said and did. The College of Bishops, the successors of the apostles, carry the same responsibility in the Church today. They are heirs and witnesses to the tradition which reaches back to the Twelve, and they pass on that teaching in its integrity to the people entrusted to their pastoral care.

Love is at the heart of this passage from St John's First Letter. Yet the kind of love of which the writer speaks is not abstract or theoretical but has its roots in the central truth of the Christian faith, the Incarnation of Jesus Christ. The supreme expression of the Father's divine love was the sending of his Son into the world. As he solemnly testified in the prologue of his letter, John again declares that he is bearing witness to what he has seen: the presence of the Word made flesh among us. To acknowledge this truth of who Jesus Christ really was draws us into the circle of the divine love, ultimately into the infinite abyss of love which is God himself. Note how John is at pains to underline the importance of doctrine in order to be caught up in this love. When we believe and confess that Jesus Christ is truly the Son of God it is then that we are transported into the reality of God's love, something which transcends our human capabilities.

[Gospel: see Wednesday of Seventh Week, p.135]

Readings: Acts 7:55-60; Apocalypse 22:12-14,16-17,20;
John 17:20-26

Both the Spirit and the bride say: Come!
Apocalypse 22:17

[First Reading: see Tuesday of Third Week, p.55]

The concluding verses of the Book of the Apocalypse express the longing of the Church for Christ to return in glory. As his bride, she earnestly awaits his coming when he will reward the saints for their righteous deeds. The first and last letters of the Greek alphabet are applied to Jesus, because through his death and resurrection he is the supreme embodiment of God's plan for the whole of creation. The apostle Paul expresses a similar vein of thought when he speaks of God 'summing up' all things in Christ (Eph 1:10). The Apocalypse as a whole is something of a mosaic of biblical quotations and allusions, often of a poetic and highly literary nature. In less elevated language, we know from the four gospels and the writings of St Paul that Christ will come again as judge. When the seer speaks of 'washing our robes clean' he is referring to a life lived as Christ taught, then we hope to be found worthy to enter the new Jerusalem. There, in contrast to our first parents banished from the Garden of Eden, we will drink the true living water and partake of the food of the tree of life. Meanwhile, the Bride of Christ waits with yearning and eager expectation for him to return and finally take her home.

[Gospel: see Thursday of Seventh Week, p.137]

By the same author and published by ST PAULS:

The Greatest of These is Love
Daily Meditations on St Paul
Michael Campbell OSA

The celebration of the 2000th anniversary of the birth of St Paul provides us with the opportunity to reflect on the character and writings of this remarkable Apostle. In *The Greatest of These is Love* Bishop Michael Campbell, with characteristic insight and lucidity, guides us day by day through a month with St Paul, with a daily reflection, meditation and prayer, based on the writings of the Apostle. Bishop Michael provides new and enriching insights into this very complex yet engaging figure. A few minutes each day spent reflecting and meditating on these inspirational texts will enable us to appreciate and make our own the thoughts, struggles and virtues of the Apostle of the Gentiles.

ISBN 978-0-85439-745-7   Hardback   £6.99

A Time to Seek the Lord

Meditations for Lent

Michael Campbell OSA

"… In this book, Fr Michael Campbell brings us back to the simple foundation of our faith. It invites us back to the essentials: how Jesus Christ speaks to us through the Scriptures – and how we may respond to His word. Drawing on the Scripture passages of Mass throughout Lent, Fr Michael's commentary draws us back to the way that God prepared His people for the coming of the Messiah and how that plan is confirmed and completed in all that Jesus teaches and does. Then, acknowledging that each Christian is called on a journey of faith which must include growth and change, the question must be 'What is my response to the Word of God?' Let us allow this Lent to speak to us of God's loving plan, and challenge us about the way we live our lives." *(Bishop John Arnold)*

ISBN 978-0-85439-740-2   Paperback   £5.99

A Shoot from the Stock of Jesse
Meditations for Advent
Michael Campbell OSA

During the season of Advent the Church sets before us a choice of Scriptural texts and antiphons to prepare us for the birthday of Christ our Saviour and Messiah. The period preceding Christmas is a busy one for many people nowadays and the spiritual dimension of Advent can easily be overlooked. In this little book the author offers us a daily Advent reflection based on one of the Scripture readings of the liturgy of the day. A few minutes of quiet reflection on the Word of God each day of Advent will lead us into a deeper understanding of the mystery of the Word made Flesh, and so make the feast of Christmas spiritually so much more meaningful.

ISBN 978-0-85439-724-2   Paperback   £4.50

Mary, Woman of Prayer
Meditations on the Mysteries of the Rosary
Michael Campbell OSA

"In this beautiful book of meditations, *Mary, Woman of Prayer,* the author has given us new and enriching reflections on the journey of faith which we each have to make. Where better to use them than during a pilgrimage to Lourdes? That holy place has been hallowed by the prayers of faithful people over the last one hundred and fifty years. As we join together in prayer on pilgrimage, the words of the preface for the Assumption of Our Lady into heaven shine light on the faith and the hope we all share. She was '…taken up to heaven to be the beginning and the pattern of the Church in its perfection, and a sign of hope and comfort for your people on their pilgrim way.'" (*Bishop George Stack*)

Illustrated with original photographs of Lourdes.

ISBN 978-0-85439-736-5   Paperback   £5.99